The Unquotable
ABRAHAM LINCOLN

～ THE LOCHLAINN SEABROOK COLLECTION ～

AMERICAN CIVIL WAR
Abraham Lincoln Was a Liberal, Jefferson Davis Was a Conservative: The Missing Key to Understanding the American Civil War
Confederacy 101: Amazing Facts You Never Knew About America's Oldest Political Tradition
Confederate Blood and Treasure: An Interview With Lochlainn Seabrook
Everything You Were Taught About African-Americans and the Civil War is Wrong, Ask a Southerner!
Everything You Were Taught About the Civil War is Wrong, Ask a Southerner!
Give This Book to a Yankee! A Southern Guide to the Civil War For Northerners
Lincoln's War: The Real Cause, the Real Winner, the Real Loser
The Great Yankee Coverup: What the North Doesn't Want You to Know About Lincoln's War!
The Ultimate Civil War Quiz Book: How Much Do You Really Know About America's Most Misunderstood Conflict?

CONFEDERATE FLAG
Confederate Flag Facts: What Every American Should Know About Dixie's Southern Cross

SECESSION
All We Ask Is To Be Let Alone: The Southern Secession Fact Book

SLAVERY
Everything You Were Taught About American Slavery is Wrong, Ask a Southerner!
Slavery 101: Amazing Facts You Never Knew About America's "Peculiar Institution"

CHILDREN
Honest Jeff and Dishonest Abe: A Southern Children's Guide to the Civil War
Saddle, Sword, and Gun: A Biography of Nathan Bedford Forrest For Teens

NATHAN BEDFORD FORREST
A Rebel Born: A Defense of Nathan Bedford Forrest - Confederate General, American Legend (winner of the 2011 Jefferson Davis Historical Gold Medal)
A Rebel Born: The Screenplay
Forrest! 99 Reasons to Love Nathan Bedford Forrest
Give 'Em Hell Boys! The Complete Military Correspondence of Nathan Bedford Forrest
Nathan Bedford Forrest and African-Americans: Yankee Myth, Confederate Fact
Nathan Bedford Forrest and the Battle of Fort Pillow: Yankee Myth, Confederate Fact
Nathan Bedford Forrest and the Ku Klux Klan: Yankee Myth, Confederate Fact
Nathan Bedford Forrest: Southern Hero, American Patriot - Honoring a Confederate Icon and the Old South
Saddle, Sword, and Gun: A Biography of Nathan Bedford Forrest For Teens
The Quotable Nathan Bedford Forrest: Selections From the Writings and Speeches of the Confederacy's Most Brilliant Cavalryman

QUOTABLE SERIES
The Alexander H. Stephens Reader: Excerpts From the Works of a Confederate Founding Father
The Quotable Alexander H. Stephens: Selections From the Writings and Speeches of the Confederacy's First Vice President
The Quotable Jefferson Davis: Selections From the Writings and Speeches of the Confederacy's First President
The Quotable Nathan Bedford Forrest: Selections From the Writings and Speeches of the Confederacy's Most Brilliant Cavalryman
The Quotable Robert E. Lee: Selections From the Writings and Speeches of the South's Most Beloved Civil War General
The Quotable Stonewall Jackson: Selections From the Writings and Speeches of the South's Most Famous General
The Unquotable Abraham Lincoln: The President's Quotes They Don't Want You To Know!

CONSTITUTIONAL HISTORY
The Articles of Confederation Explained: A Clause-by-Clause Study of America's First Constitution
The Constitution of the Confederate States of America Explained: A Clause-by-Clause Study of the South's Magna Carta

VICTORIAN CONFEDERATE LITERATURE
Rise Up and Call Them Blessed: Victorian Tributes to the Confederate Soldier, 1861-1901
The Old Rebel: Robert E. Lee As He Was Seen By His Contemporaries
Victorian Confederate Poetry: The Southern Cause in Verse, 1861-1901

ABRAHAM LINCOLN
Abraham Lincoln: The Southern View - Demythologizing America's Sixteenth President
Lincolnology: The Real Abraham Lincoln Revealed in His Own Words - A Study of Lincoln's Suppressed, Misinterpreted, and Forgotten Writings and Speeches
The Great Impersonator! 99 Reasons to Dislike Abraham Lincoln
The Unholy Crusade: Lincoln's Legacy of Destruction in the American South
The Unquotable Abraham Lincoln: The President's Quotes They Don't Want You To Know!

CIVIL WAR BATTLES
Encyclopedia of the Battle of Franklin - A Comprehensive Guide to the Conflict that Changed the Civil War
Nathan Bedford Forrest and the Battle of Fort Pillow: Yankee Myth, Confederate Fact

PARANORMAL
Carnton Plantation Ghost Stories: True Tales of the Unexplained from Tennessee's Most Haunted Civil War House!
UFOs and Aliens: The Complete Guidebook

FAMILY HISTORIES
The Blakeneys: An Etymological, Ethnological, and Genealogical Study - Uncovering the Mysterious Origins of the Blakeney Family and Name
The Caudills: An Etymological, Ethnological, and Genealogical Study - Exploring the Name and National Origins of a European-American Family
The McGavocks of Carnton Plantation: A Southern History - Celebrating One of Dixie's Most Noble Confederate Families and Their Tennessee Home

MIND, BODY, SPIRIT
Autobiography of a Non-Yogi: A Scientist's Journey From Hinduism to Christianity (Dr. Amitava Dasgupta, with Lochlainn Seabrook)
Britannia Rules: Goddess-Worship in Ancient Anglo-Celtic Society - An Academic Look at the United Kingdom's Matricentric Spiritual Past
Christ Is All and In All: Rediscovering Your Divine Nature and the Kingdom Within
Christmas Before Christianity: How the Birthday of the "Sun" Became the Birthday of the "Son"
Jesus and the Gospel of Q: Christ's Pre-Christian Teachings As Recorded in the New Testament
Jesus and the Law of Attraction: The Bible-Based Guide to Creating Perfect Health, Wealth, and Happiness Following Christ's Simple Formula
Seabrook's Bible Dictionary of Traditional and Mystical Christian Doctrines
The Bible and the Law of Attraction: 99 Teachings of Jesus, the Apostles, and the Prophets
The Book of Kelle: An Introduction to Goddess-Worship and the Great Celtic Mother-Goddess Kelle, Original Blessed Lady of Ireland
The Goddess Dictionary of Words and Phrases: Introducing a New Core Vocabulary for the Women's Spirituality Movement
The Way of Holiness: The Story of Religion and Myth From the Cave Bear Cult to Christianity

WOMEN
Aphrodite's Trade: The Hidden History of Prostitution Unveiled
Princess Diana: Modern Day Moon-Goddess - A Psychoanalytical and Mythological Look at Diana Spencer's Life, Marriage, and Death (with Dr. Jane Goldberg)
Women in Gray: A Tribute to the Ladies Who Supported the Southern Confederacy

Five-Star Books & Gifts From the Heart of the American South
SeaRavenPress.com

The Unquotable
ABRAHAM LINCOLN

The President's Quotes They Don't Want You To Know!

COLLECTED, ARRANGED, & EDITED, WITH AN INTRODUCTION & NOTES, BY
"THE VOICE OF THE TRADITIONAL SOUTH" COLONEL
LOCHLAINN SEABROOK
JEFFERSON DAVIS HISTORICAL GOLD MEDAL WINNER

Diligently Researched and Generously Illustrated for the Elucidation of the Reader

2018
Sea Raven Press, Nashville, Tennessee, USA

THE UNQUOTABLE ABRAHAM LINCOLN

Published by
Sea Raven Press, Cassidy Ravensdale, President
PO Box 1484, Spring Hill, Tennessee 37174-1484 USA
SeaRavenPress.com • searavenpress@gmail.com

Copyright © 2011-2018 Lochlainn Seabrook
in accordance with U.S. and international copyright laws and regulations, as stated and protected under the Berne Union for the Protection of Literary and Artistic Property (Berne Convention), and the Universal Copyright Convention (the UCC). All rights reserved under the Pan-American and International Copyright Conventions.

1st SRP paperback edition, 1st printing October 2011; 2nd printing January 2018: ISBN: 978-0-9838185-2-6
1st SRP hardcover edition, 1st printing January 2016; 2nd printing January 2018: ISBN: 978-1-943737-18-5

ISBN: 978-0-9838185-2-6 (paperback)
Library of Congress Control Number: 2011937364

This work is the copyrighted intellectual property of Lochlainn Seabrook and has been registered with the Copyright Office at the Library of Congress in Washington, D.C., USA. No part of this work (including text, covers, drawings, photos, illustrations, maps, images, diagrams, etc.), in whole or in part, may be used, reproduced, stored in a retrieval system, or transmitted, in any form or by any means now known or hereafter invented, without written permission from the publisher. The sale, duplication, hire, lending, copying, digitalization, or reproduction of this material, in any manner or form whatsoever, is also prohibited, and is a violation of federal, civil, and digital copyright law, which provides severe civil and criminal penalties for any violations.

The Unquotable Abraham Lincoln: The President's Quotes They Don't Want You To Know!, collected and edited, with an introduction and notes, by Lochlainn Seabrook. Includes bibliographical references.

Front & back cover design & art, book design, layout, & interior art by Lochlainn Seabrook
All images, graphic design, graphic art, & illustrations copyright © Lochlainn Seabrook
All images selected, placed, manipulated, and/or created by Lochlainn Seabrook
Front cover sketch: "Abraham Lincoln" copyright © Chris Rommel
Cover images & design copyright © Lochlainn Seabrook

The views on the American "Civil War" documented in this book are those of the publisher.

PRINTED & MANUFACTURED IN OCCUPIED TENNESSEE, FORMER CONFEDERATE STATES OF AMERICA

Dedication

To those who – unlike Lincoln – honor truth, respect all God's children, and believe in the U.S. Constitution.

Epigraph

"I meant all I said, and did not
mean anything I did not say."

Abraham Lincoln
February 14, 1860

CONTENTS

Notes to the Reader - 10
Introduction, by Lochlainn Seabrook - 13
Historical Time Line - 16

1 THE U.S. PRESIDENCY - 19
2 THE U.S. GOVERNMENT - 24
3 THE U.S. CONSTITUTION - 27
4 SECESSION & STATES' RIGHTS - 30
5 THE UNION - 37
6 THE CAUSE & PURPOSE OF THE WAR - 40
7 ABOLITION - 46
8 SLAVERY - 56
9 THE GETTYSBURG ADDRESS - 73
10 THE SOUTHERN PEOPLE - 75
11 AFRICAN AMERICANS & WHITE RACISM - 77
12 BLACK EQUAL RIGHTS - 88
13 BLACK COLONIZATION & AND WHITE SEPARATISM - 92
14 THE EMANCIPATION PROCLAMATION - 110
15 LINCOLN'S WAR ON THE SOUTH - 119
16 LINCOLN'S WAR ON THE NORTH - 121
17 LINCOLN'S WAR CRIMES - 124
18 RELIGION - 128
19 QUOTABLE QUOTES ABOUT LINCOLN - 131

Notes - 133
Bibliography - 142
Meet the Author - 146
Meet the Cover Artist - 148

～ Notes to the Reader ～

A WORD ON EARLY AMERICAN MATERIAL
☙ In an effort to retain the true character and meaning of Abraham Lincoln's words, they have been printed here exactly as they appear in the original manuscripts, including typographical and grammatical peculiarities inherent to 19th-Century Southern writing and speaking. Lincoln's quotes are marked with a traditional Victorian hand pointer. My chapter introductions are in normal font, my explanatory comments appear in italics above Lincoln's quotes, and my clarifications are in brackets within his quotes.

THE TWO MAIN POLITICAL PARTIES IN 1860
☙ In any study of the "Civil War" it is vitally important to keep in mind that the two major political parties were then the opposite of what they are today. The Democrats of the 19th Century were Conservatives, akin to the Republican Party of today, while the Republicans of the 19th Century were Liberals, akin to the Democratic Party of today. Thus the Confederacy's Democratic president, Jefferson Davis, was a Conservative (with libertarian leanings); the Union's Republican president, Abraham Lincoln, was a Liberal (with socialistic leanings). For a detailed discussion of this topic, see my book, *Abraham Lincoln Was a Liberal, Jefferson Davis Was a Conservative: The Missing Key to Understanding the American Civil War*.

THE PENULTIMATE DEMAGOGUE ABRAHAM LINCOLN
☙ One may wonder, after perusing Lincoln's quotes, why I, the editor, found it necessary to intrude with my own explanations.

When writing about Lincoln one is always faced with two serious problems: his murky often completely unintelligible writing and, more importantly, his overt demagoguery and unconstrained duplicity. In plain English, he said one thing to his Northern audiences and quite another to his Southern audiences, often purposefully using wording meant to confuse. His critics complained loudly and often about his muddy writing style and barefaced political hypocrisy, which the slick politician duly ignored.

One of the most vociferous from this category was Lincoln's senatorial opponent, Stephen A. Douglas, who once said in a speech:

> "My friend Lincoln finds it extremely difficult to manage a debate in the central part of the State, where there is a mixture of men from the North and the South. In the extreme northern part of Illinois he can proclaim as bold and radical Abolitionism as ever [Joshua R.] Giddings, [Elijah P.] Lovejoy, or [William Lloyd] Garrison enunciated; but when he gets down a little further south he claims that he is an old-line Whig, a disciple of Henry Clay, and declares that he still adheres to the old-line Whig creed, and has nothing whatever to do with Abolitionism, or negro equality, or negro citizenship."[1]

Let us look an example of what Douglas is referring to.

On July 10, 1858, at Chicago, Illinois, Lincoln said the following:

> "I should like to know if, taking this old Declaration of Independence, which declares that all men are equal upon principle, and making exceptions to it, where will it stop? If one man says it does not mean a negro, why may not another man say it does not mean another man? If the Declaration is not the truth, let us get the statute-book in which we find it and tear it out. Who is so bold as to do it? If it is not true, let us tear it out."[2]

Now let us look at an excerpt from a September 18, 1858, speech that he gave further south, in Charleston, Illinois, where his white constituents happened to be less racially tolerant:

> "I will say, then, that I am not nor ever have been in favor of bringing about in any way the social and political equality of the white and black races; that I am not nor ever have been in favor of making voters of the free negroes, or jurors, or qualifying them to hold office, or having them to marry with white people. . . . I as much as any other man am in favor of the superior position being assigned to the white man."[3]

There are two opposing Lincolns on display here, both trying desperately to curry votes from two different groups of people. But only one of them can be the real Lincoln. Which one is it? As we will see, it is the second one who turns out to be authentic.

It is due to the inevitable confusion stemming from this type of double-dealing dishonesty—which Lincoln evinced throughout his entire political career—that most of his quotes require some interpretation.

LEARN MORE
&⋆ Lincoln's War on the American people and the Constitution can never be fully understood without a thorough knowledge of the South's perspective. As this book is only meant to be a brief introductory guide to these topics, one cannot hope to learn the complete story here. For those who are interested in additional material from Dixie's viewpoint, please see my comprehensive histories listed on pages 2 and 3.

For those seeking a more in-depth study of Lincoln specifically, see my additional books on America's 16th chief executive:
- *Abraham Lincoln: The Southern View - Demythologizing America's Sixteenth President*
- *Lincoln's War: The Real Cause, the Real Winner, the Real Loser*
- *The Great Impersonator: 99 Reasons to Dislike Abraham Lincoln*
- *The Unholy Crusade: Lincoln's Legacy of Destruction in the American South*
- *Lincolnology: The Real Abraham Lincoln Revealed in His Own Words - A Study of Lincoln's Suppressed, Misinterpreted, and Forgotten Speeches and Writings*

Keep Your Body, Mind, & Spirit Vibrating at Their Highest Level

YOU CAN DO SO BY READING THE BOOKS OF

SEA RAVEN PRESS

There is nothing that will so perfectly keep your body, mind, and spirit in a healthy condition as to think wisely and positively. Hence you should not only read this book, but also the other books that we offer. They will quicken your physical, mental, and spiritual vibrations, enabling you to maintain a position in society as a healthy erudite person.

KEEP YOURSELF WELL-INFORMED!

The well-informed person is always at the head of the procession, while the ignorant, the lazy, and the unthoughtful hang onto the rear. If you are a Spiritual man or woman, do yourself a great favor: read Sea Raven Press books and stay well posted on the Truth. It is almost criminal for one to remain in ignorance while the opportunity to gain knowledge is open to all at a nominal price.

We invite you to visit our Webstore for a wide selection of wholesome, family-friendly, well-researched, educational books for all ages. You will be glad you did!

Five-Star Books & Gifts From the Heart of the American South

SeaRavenPress.com

INTRODUCTION

IF WE ARE TO BELIEVE the nearly 20,000 books written by pro-North historians about Abraham Lincoln, not only has he always been America's favorite president, he was an ardent abolitionist, Bible-believing Christian, and Constitution-loving Conservative who headed the most ethical administration in history, preserved the Union, ended American slavery, and became the black man's greatest champion by granting him full civil and equal rights.

In fact, according to Lincoln's own words, nothing could be further from the truth. His writings reveal a man who openly detested abolitionists and deemed abolition a greater evil than slavery.[4] Far from being a Christian, he was a lifelong atheist who scoffed at the Bible,[5] referred to Jesus as a "bastard,"[6] and labeled Christians "ignoramuses."[7]

In this brief study of some of the president's lesser known quotes, the authentic Abraham Lincoln—long hidden by pro-Lincoln scholars and writers—will be revealed. One of the facts that they would rather you not know is that he was a white separatist who campaigned throughout his entire life for American apartheid.

Though a Republican, he was no Conservative, for in the mid 19th Century the platforms of the Republicans and Democrats were reversed.[8] His own writings tell us that he was a big government, big spending Liberal with socialist leanings, a left-wing ideologue with dictatorial tendencies who did not like the Constitution and never hesitated to walk over it, ignore it completely, or even reinterpret it to fit his own political agenda.

Far from running an ethical presidency, objective constitutional and legal scholars refer to the Lincoln administration as the lowest period for civil liberties up to that time. Some actually rank it as one of the worst in all of American history.[9]

Despite the modern deification of our sixteenth president, during his two terms in office he was extremely disliked in both the North and the South.[10] Indeed, not only was Ulysses S. Grant far more popular,[11] in the 1860s a large percentage of the general public viewed Lincoln as the worst chief executive up to that time,[12] some even referring to him as "America's most hated president."[13]

As for "preserving the Union," Lincoln's writings show that he instead destroyed it, for he turned what the Founding Fathers intended to be a "voluntary Union of friendly states," as Jefferson Davis put it,[14] into an involuntary Union of states "pinned to the residue with bayonets," as Yankee abolitionist Horace Greeley phrased it.[15]

Was Lincoln the "Great Emancipator"? Did he truly "free the slaves" with the Final Emancipation Proclamation, issued January 1, 1863, as we have been reverently told for the past 150 years? Not according to authentic history. Slavery ended with the ratification of the Thirteenth Amendment in December 1865, eight months *after* Lincoln died in April of that year. And according to Lincoln's own pen his intent was never complete abolition, for throughout the Civil War he repeatedly told the South it could keep slavery for all he cared, as long as the seceded states returned to the Union[16] and paid their taxes.[17] He was, after all, a strong supporter of the Corwin Amendment (which would have allowed slavery to continue in perpetuity)—a well-known fact that he brought up in his First Inaugural Speech on March 4, 1861.[18]

As Lincoln himself said, his main interest in regards to slavery was always to restrict it to the South, prevent its spread into the new Western states, and prohibit it from reestablishing itself in the North[19]—where it had got its start in the 1600s.[20]

As will be shown, John Wilkes Booth was the true "Great Emancipator."

Finally, pro-North historians would like us to believe that Lincoln was our nation's greatest benefactor of African-Americans and a leading proponent of black equal rights. Was he?

From the president's own surviving works we discover that he was actually a white supremacist, a white separatist, and a black colonizationist; one who did not hesitate to use the "n" word, who considered blacks an "inferior race," and whose number one goal was to create a black-free America that was white from coast to coast. This was to be accomplished, as he put it, by "sending all blacks back to their native land."[21] If deportation was not feasible, then Lincoln hoped that American blacks could at least be set up in their own all-black state, preferably far from his adopted home state, Illinois.[22]

Why are these stunning facts not better known? It is because nearly everything Lincoln wrote or said that is considered politically incorrect or which challenges the long cherished Northern view of the Civil War, has been suppressed by die-hard Lincolnites, those faithful, impossibly sentimental, and often history ignorant members of the Lincolnian Church.

Not all of Lincoln's controversial words have been purposefully ignored or buried, however. Before he left Illinois for the White House in early 1861, Lincoln himself destroyed untold numbers of his own papers. His friends contributed to the destruction of the Lincoln literary corpus by giving many of his writings away as souvenirs. Even his house servants played a role: one mistook several piles of his valuable notes for garbage and threw them into the fire.[23]

One of Lincoln's early employer's destroyed what must rank as one of history's most fascinating but unknown works, a "little book" that the future president wrote to promote his virulent anti-Christian beliefs. According to the many people who read it before it went up in flames, Lincoln held that the Bible is a work of fairy tales, Jesus is not the Son of God, and miracles are a scientific impossibility.[24]

Worst of all was Lincoln's son Robert Todd Lincoln. In the early 1900s, after the death of his father's official biographers, John Nicolay and John Hay, Robert took over ownership of what little remained of the president's writings and burned everything that he felt cast his dad in a negative light. One person who witnessed this travesty of history said that when he walked into the room, Robert was sitting on the floor throwing sheets of paper into the fireplace as fast as he could.[25]

Though thousands, perhaps tens of thousands, of pages of Lincoln's original writings have been obliterated, enough remain for us to get at the real man. This book contains pertinent examples of these surviving documents.

The president's son, Robert Todd Lincoln, intentionally burned thousands of his father's papers. Why?

As a Southerner who lost ancestors due to Lincoln and his illegal, reckless, and unnecessary war on the South, I have not one jot of love for our sixteenth chief executive. On the other hand, as a Christian I do not wish to foment hatred of him.

The goal of this book—as is true of all my books on him—is to tear away the shadowy veil of mythology that now surrounds him, and allow the world to glimpse the genuine person. Not according to my personal views, but according to the pen of Abraham Lincoln, for no one could ever convey his true inner character as well as he himself did.

Many would prefer that these quotes never be seen by the public, hence the title of this book: *The Unquotable Abraham Lincoln*. However, I, like most other Southerners and lovers of liberty, think that "Honest Abe's" unquotable quotes should be cited and studied as much as possible.

After 150 years of being subjected to coverups, silly myths, impossible romanticizations, outright lies, and mountains of anti-South Civil War propaganda regarding "Honest Abe," it is high time to let his old marbleized facade crumble and fall away. For the so-called "Civil War," even much of American history itself, cannot be fully understood without a thorough knowledge of who Lincoln really was and what he really believed.

Lochlainn Seabrook
Franklin, Williamson County, Tennessee, USA
September 2011

Historical Time Line

1809 - Lincoln is born February 12 at Hodgenville, Hardin (now Larue) County, Kentucky.
1816 - Lincoln's father moves his family to Indiana.
1830 - Lincoln's father moves his family to Illinois on March 1.
1832 - On April 19 Lincoln enlists in the Illinois Militia.
1833 - Lincoln is appointed postmaster on May 7 at New Salem, Illinois.
1835 - Lincoln serves in Illinois General Assembly for one year beginning December 7.
1837 - Lincoln moves to Springfield, Illinois and becomes a lawyer.
1842 - Lincoln marries Mary Todd on November 4 at Springfield, Illinois (4 children).
1847 - Lincoln, a Whig (Liberal), serves as an Illinois Representative for two years beginning March 4.
1856 - On June 19 Lincoln loses his bid to become the Republican (then the Liberal) vice presidential nominee.
1858 - From August 21 to October 15, Lincoln holds seven debates with his Democratic (Conservative) opponent Stephen A. Douglas.
1858 - On November 2 Lincoln loses his bid to become an Illinois senator.
1860 - On May 18 Lincoln is nominated to become the Republican (Liberal) presidential candidate.
1860 - On November 6 big government Liberal Lincoln is "elected" U.S. president with a minority of the popular vote in the North and with no votes in the Conservative South.
1861 - Lincoln is inaugurated March 4 at Washington, D.C. and enters the White House.
1861 - On April 12 Lincoln devilishly tricks the South into firing the first shot at the Battle of Fort Sumter, opening the so-called "Civil War."
1862 - On September 22 Lincoln issues his Preliminary Emancipation Proclamation, which calls for continued efforts to deport all blacks out of the U.S.
1863 - On January 1, in a diabolical attempt to start a massive slave insurrection across the South and replace his depleted white troops, Lincoln issues his Final Emancipation Proclamation, but only in regions of the South that have not been conquered by U.S. troops. Slavery in the North, and in those sections of the South that have been defeated, is, in Lincoln's own words, to be "left as if this Proclamation were not issued." The Emancipation Proclamation—which he wrote out purely as a "military necessity" and a "war measure" (in his words)—pleases no one, there is no slave insurrection anywhere in the Confederacy, and not one slave is freed. However, the edict serves its true purpose: Lincoln later claimed that without the 200,000 blacks who entered the Union army (thousands who were coerced at gunpoint), he could not have won his war.
1863 - On November 19 Lincoln delivers his infamous hypocritical anti-South speech, the Gettysburg Address, in an effort to maintain Northern support for his war.
1864 - On November 8 Lincoln is "elected" to a second term as U.S. President using bribery, horse-trading, threats, patronage, and double-dealing. To assure a win, he also rigs the election by stationing his soldiers at the polls to intimidate voters.
1865 - Lincoln is inaugurated March 4 at Washington, D.C. for his second term.
1865 - On April 9 Confederate General Robert E. Lee "surrenders" at Appomattox, Virginia, ending the War for Southern Independence. Lee later mournfully regrets the decision. So-called "Reconstruction" begins, a naked attempt to both Northernize and punish the South; in reality, a "second Civil War," as Southerners referred to it.
1865 - Lincoln is shot by John Wilkes Booth on April 14 at Ford's Theater, Washington, D.C.
1865 - Lincoln dies from his wound April 15; his funeral is held at the White House on the 19th.
1865 - Lincoln is buried on May 4 at Oak Ridge Cemetery, Springfield, Illinois.
1865 - On December 6 American slavery is finally eradicated with the ratification of the Thirteenth Amendment, eight months *after* Lincoln's death.

The Unquotable
ABRAHAM
LINCOLN

THE PRESIDENT'S QUOTES
THEY DON'T WANT YOU TO KNOW!

THE U.S. PRESIDENCY

FOR AN INDIVIDUAL TO BECOME America's chief executive in the 21st Century, he or she must have a strong, positive, and healthy self-image, all traits which were lacking in Abraham Lincoln. You are not supposed to know about the following quotes, for they prove irrefutably that he would not have been elected president had he lived today.

Lincoln's 1859 reply to an Illinois newspaper editor who suggested he make a run for the White House:
☞ ". . . I must in candor say I do not think myself fit for the presidency. I certainly am flattered and gratified that some partial friends think of me in that connection; but I really think it best for our cause that no concerted effort, such as you suggest, should be made."[26]

During a causal 1858 conversation with German immigrant Henry Villard:
☞ "I did not consider myself qualified for the United States Senate, and it took me a long time to persuade myself that I was. Now, to be sure I am convinced that I am good enough for it; but, in spite of it all, I am saying to myself every day: 'It is too big a thing for you; you will never get it.' [My wife] Mary insists, however, that I am going to be Senator and President of the United States, too. Just think of such a sucker as me as President!"[27]

After losing the 1858 Illinois senatorial race to incumbent Stephen A. Douglas:
☞ ". . . I now sink out of view, and shall be forgotten."[28]

Even after he became president, the solitary, secretive, melancholy, and largely friendless Lincoln continued to belittle himself and his abilities, in part because of the abysmal manner in which his political associates treated him, as he once complained to Ward Hill Lamon:

☞ "I wish I had never been born! I would rather be dead than as President thus abused in the house of my friends."[29]

Upon hearing the news that he had been nominated for U.S. president in the spring of 1860:

☞ "[I am deeply] and even painfully sensible of the great responsibility which is inseparable from this high honor—a responsibility which I could almost wish had fallen upon some one of the far more eminent men and experienced statesmen whose distinguished names were before the convention . . ."[30]

In the summer of 1864 Lincoln wrote out this "Reply to a Delegation from the National Union League" regarding his renomination for the upcoming election that year:

☞ "Gentlemen: I can only say in response to the kind remarks of your chairman, as I suppose, that I am very grateful for the renewed confidence which has been accorded to me both by the convention and by the National League. I am not insensible at all to the personal compliment there is in this, and yet I do not allow myself to believe that any but a small portion of it is to be appropriated as a personal compliment. That really the convention and the Union League assembled with a higher view—that of taking care of the interests of the country for the present and the great future—and that the part I am entitled to appropriate as a compliment is only that part which I may lay hold of as being the opinion of the convention and of the League, that I am not entirely unworthy to be intrusted with the place which I have occupied for the last three years. But I do not allow myself to suppose that either the convention or the League have concluded to decide that I am either the greatest or best man in America, but rather they have concluded that it is not best to swap horses while crossing the river, and have further concluded that I am not so poor a horse that they might not make a botch of it in trying to swap."[31]

From Lincoln's February 18, 1861, address to the New York Legislature at Albany:
☞ "I hold myself, without mock modesty, the humblest of all individuals that have ever been elevated to the presidency . . ."[32]

During his February 19, 1861, speech at Poughkeepsie, New York, Lincoln made this comment concerning his November 1860 election to the presidency:
☞ "I do not say that in the recent election the people did the wisest thing that could have been done; indeed, I do not think they did; but I do say that in accepting the great trust committed to me, which I do with a determination to endeavor to prove worthy of it, I must rely upon you, upon the people of the whole country, for support . . ."[33]

In a written February 20, 1861, reply to New York Mayor Fernando Wood on becoming president of the United States:
☞ "I fear too great confidence may have been placed in me."[34]

How did Lincoln really view himself? This excerpt from an April 1, 1838, letter to Eliza Caldwell Browning, the wife of Orville Hickman Browning, gives us a clue:
☞ "I have now come to the conclusion never again to think of marrying, and for this reason—I can never be satisfied with any one who would be blockhead enough to have me."[35]

In 1864 Lincoln was asked what he thought of the anti-Lincoln Wade-Davis Bill, as well as a scathing speech by his arch critic abolitionist Wendell Phillips:
☞ "No, I have not seen them, nor do I care to see them. I have seen enough to satisfy me that I am a failure, not only in the opinion of the people in rebellion [that is, Southerners], but of many distinguished politicians of my own party."[36]

Not long after he became president, Lincoln's self-image changed dramatically. Once a self-effacing and humble man who supported the idea of states' rights, he quickly came to believe that he was an omnipotent king-like ruler who possessed sweeping dictatorial powers over the entire U.S., powers the Constitution clearly did not grant him. On February 17, 1864, for instance, after being told about some minor political dissension among Arkansas' citizens, a newly despotic Lincoln made the following statement. How would Americans today feel if our current president made this same remark?

☞ "This discord must be silenced."[37]

Lincoln was one of our most psychologically and emotionally detached presidents. Here, for example, is what he had to say on February 13, 1861, on the eve of America's bloodiest and most violent home war, and with seven Southern states having already seceded:

☞ "I have not maintained silence from any want of real anxiety. It is a good thing that there is no more than anxiety, for there is nothing going wrong. It is a consoling circumstance that when we look out there is nothing that really hurts anybody. We entertain different views upon political questions, but nobody is suffering anything. This is a most consoling circumstance, and from it we may conclude that all we want is time, patience, and a reliance on that God who has never forsaken this people."[38]

Only a few days later, on February 15, 1861, at Pittsburgh, Pennsylvania, Lincoln made this astonishing remark:

☞ "Notwithstanding the troubles across the river [Lincoln points southward across the Monongahela River, and smiles], there is no crisis but an artificial one. What is there now to warrant the condition of affairs presented by our friends [that is, Southerners] over the river? Take even their own view of the questions involved, and there is nothing to justify the course they are pursuing [that is, secession]. I repeat, then, there is no crisis, excepting such a one as may be gotten up at any time by turbulent men aided by designing politicians. My advice to them, under such circumstances, is to keep cool."[39]

Such comments did nothing to inspire confidence in Lincoln's leadership. In fact, it only made the American people even more doubtful of his ability to head the United States of America, particularly in times of crisis. Had they known the real Lincoln, however, such statements would not have surprised anyone. Here, for instance, is what he said in a speech that was quoted in New York newspapers on October 10, 1864, four years into his war on the South:

☞ "I am not controlling events, but events are controlling me."⁴⁰

Lincoln was highly aware of his power as president, particularly when it came to spreading anti-South propaganda, a practice that helped him justify his unjustifiable war on the South. This sort of thing came quite naturally to him, for as a former newspaper agent and journalist (for the Springfield, Illinois, Sangamon Journal) and a newspaper owner (of the Illinois Staats-Anzeiger), he was adept at using the press to shape public opinion. Little wonder then that newspaperman Lincoln often used and manipulated both the public and the media; not only to assist with his own political aspirations, but in aiding and abetting the creation of what is now a large corpus of spurious anti-South myths.⁴¹ Well aware of his power over public opinion, and sounding very much like a ruthless dictator, here is how he expressed it on August 21, 1858:

Lincoln did not believe he should have been made president of the U.S. We in the South agree.

☞ ". . . public sentiment is everything. With public sentiment, nothing can fail; without it, nothing can succeed. Consequently he who molds public sentiment goes deeper than he who enacts statutes or pronounces decisions. He makes statutes and decisions possible or impossible to be executed."⁴²

THE U.S. GOVERNMENT

BECAUSE HE DEPLORED THE U.S. Constitution (in particular the Ninth and Tenth Amendments), Lincoln felt he could overlook it, or worse, trample it underfoot. As such, he far overstepped the boundaries set down in that document concerning the office of chief executive.[43] In fact, his ascension to the White House seemed to fill him with a dictatorial ambition that America has not seen in any president, before or since, as the following words reveal. For Lincoln, like many Liberals then as today, heading the U.S. government was not about advancing the country. It was about advancing his own personal ideals and establishing his left-wing agenda.

―――

Hints of what was to turn out to be Lincoln's burning desire to alter (that is, enlarge) the U.S. government and his near total disregard for our nation's most hallowed document, the U.S. Constitution, were evident early in his political career. On December 10, 1856, for instance, during an address at a Republican banquet in Chicago, he said:

☞ "Our government rests in public opinion. Whoever can change public opinion can change the government . . ."[44]

―――

Lincoln's war on the South itself was, in great part, not only his attempt to destroy states' rights, but also his desire to expand both the central government and his own powers as president. During his December 6, 1864, "Annual Message to Congress," Lincoln responded to pressure from his antiwar critics (who wanted the conflict halted immediately) this way:

☞ "The Executive power itself would be greatly diminished by the cessation of actual war."⁴⁵

Being a progressive, Lincoln was obsessed with the idea of complete governmental control—or "national supremacy," as he called it—over the people, as he noted in his November 20, 1863, letter to Edward Everett:

☞ "The point made against the theory of the general government being only an agency, whose principles are the States, was new to me, and, as I think, is one of the best arguments for the national supremacy."⁴⁶

Several years before his war on the South and states' rights, Lincoln let it be known that to attain full "national supremacy" he was more than willing to use physical violence, as he intimated in a June 26, 1857, speech at Springfield, Illinois:

☞ "If it prove to be true, as is probable, that the people of Utah are in open rebellion to the United States . . . I say . . they ought to be somehow coerced to obedience . . ."⁴⁷

As president three years later, Lincoln proved that he had risen to the level of dictator, when, for example, in the spring of 1861 he authorized a May 27 letter to Union General William Selby Harney of Missouri, that contained the following statement:

☞ "The authority of the United States is paramount, and whenever it is apparent that a movement, whether by color of State authority or not, is hostile, you will not hesitate to put it down."⁴⁸

As a socialistic politician, President Lincoln was wholly against states' rights, an un-American stance that put him in direct opposition to the South. The South held that each state had the right to decide for itself what was to be allowed within its borders and what was to be prohibited. Lincoln believed the opposite. For him the central government was an all-powerful body meant to rule, not only across all of the individual states, but over every aspect of human life as well. Naturally, he extended this absurd, non-existent, and unconstitutional power to the slavery issue, as he did during a speech at Cincinnati, Ohio, on September 17, 1859:

☛ "I have taken upon myself, in the name of some of you, to say that we [Liberals] expect upon these principles to ultimately beat them [the Conservatives, in the next election]. In order to do so, I think we want and must have a national policy in regard to the institution of slavery that acknowledges and deals with that institution as being wrong. Nothing will make you successful but setting up a policy which shall treat the thing as being wrong. When I say this, I do not mean to say that this General Government is charged with the duty of redressing or preventing all the wrongs in the world; but I do think that it is charged with preventing and redressing all wrongs which are wrongs to itself. This government is expressly charged with the duty of providing for the general welfare. We believe that the spreading out and perpetuity of the institution of slavery impairs the general welfare. . . . To repress this thing, we think, is providing for the general welfare."[49]

Though Lincoln was a Republican, due to the 19th-Century party reversal he was actually a Big Brother, big spending Liberal who believed that the central government was better at running the lives of the American people than they were themselves.

Based on the Ninth and Tenth Amendments, as well as Article 4, Section 4 of the U.S. Constitution,[50] Conservatives, then as today, correctly maintain that the individual states are meant to control their own affairs, not the central government at Washington, D.C. Here, however, is Liberal Lincoln's idea of the role of the central government, from a proposed speech composed around July 1, 1854:

☛ "The legitimate object of [the Federal] government is 'to do for the people what needs to be done, but which they can not, by individual effort, do at all, or do so well, for themselves.' There are many such things—some of them exist independently of the injustice in the world. Making and maintaining roads, bridges, and the like; providing for the helpless young and afflicted; common schools; and disposing of deceased men's property, are instances."[51]

THE U.S. CONSTITUTION

AT HIS INAUGURATION ON MARCH 4, 1861, Lincoln swore to uphold the U.S. Constitution. But did he? In this chapter, using quotes they would rather you not know, we will explore his true feelings about our country's most important and sacred political document.

As he did with so many other aspects of government, Lincoln completely altered his views of the U.S. Constitution after becoming president. Prior to moving into the White House he seemed to support it. Afterward he became its most boisterous enemy. Here, for example, from a June 20, 1848, address before the House of Representatives, is a comment Lincoln made concerning tampering with the Constitution:

☞ "As a general rule, I think we would much better let it alone. No slight occasion should tempt us to touch it. Better not take the first step, which may lead to a habit of altering it. Better, rather, habituate ourselves to think of it as unalterable. It can scarcely be made better than it is. New provisions would introduce new difficulties, and thus create and increase appetite for further change. No, sir; let it stand as it is. New hands have never touched it. The men who made it have done their work, and have passed away. Who shall improve on what they did?"[52]

On October 16, 1854, Lincoln stated in a public speech:

☞ "... I do not, for that cause [that is, the Three-fifths Clause, in which five black slaves were congressionally counted as being equal to three whites],[53] or any other cause, propose to destroy, or alter, or disregard the constitution. I stand to it, fairly, fully, and firmly."[54]

When Lincoln accepted his nomination for U.S. president in the spring of 1860, he swore that he would give "due regard" to states' rights and the Constitution. Here is how he phrased it in a letter to George Ashmun on May 23. These words would prove to be hollow, and short-lived:

☞ "Sir: I accept the nomination tendered me by the convention over which you presided, and of which I am formally apprised in the letter of yourself and others, acting as a committee of the convention for that purpose.

"The declaration of principles and sentiments which accompanies your letter meets my approval; and it shall be my care not to violate or disregard it in any part.

"Imploring the assistance of Divine Providence, and with due regard to the views and feelings of all who were represented in the convention—to the rights of all the States and Territories and people of the nation; to the inviolability of the Constitution; and the perpetual union, harmony, and prosperity of all—I am most happy to cooperate for the practical success of the principles declared by the convention.

"Your obliged friend and fellow-citizen, A. Lincoln."[55]

Yet, three years earlier, on June 26, 1857, during a speech at Springfield, Illinois, Lincoln quoted President Andrew Jackson with this ominous remark:

☞ ". . . hear General Jackson: 'Each public officer who takes an oath to support the Constitution swears that he will support it as he understands it, and not as it is understood by others.'"[56]

Not long after this statement, Lincoln gave a speech on September 15, 1858, at Jonesboro, Illinois, in which he said:

☞ ". . . although it is distasteful to me, I have sworn to support the Constitution."[57]

Indeed, after being elected president in November 1860, his words took on a more aggressive and sinister tone regarding the Constitution. In February 1861, while meeting with a Southern peace commission at Willard's Hotel in Washington, D.C., the president-elect was asked by New York businessman William E. Dodge what he was going to do to prevent war with the South. Lincoln's response is chilling, for it spells out his opinion of the Constitution that our Founding Fathers so painstakingly and lovingly created. When I get to the Oval Office, he said:

☞ "I shall take an oath to the best of my ability to preserve, protect, and defend the Constitution. This is a great and solemn duty. With the support of the people and the assistance of the Almighty I shall undertake to perform it. I have full faith that I shall perform it. *It is not the Constitution as I would like to have it*, but as it is that is to be defended [emphasis added]."⁵⁸

Liberal Lincoln greatly abhorred the U.S. Constitution, as his own writings and his many unconstitutional acts attest.

Though after 1860 Lincoln proclaimed a well publicized hatred of the constitutional idea of states' rights, he could still openly lie to the American public with statements such as the following, made on February 22, 1861:

☞ "I have never had a feeling, politically, that did not spring from the sentiments embodied in the Declaration of Independence."⁵⁹

In fact, on March 4, 1861, during his inauguration, Lincoln pledged to uphold the Constitution by repeating this oath aloud:

☞ "I do solemnly swear (or affirm) that I will faithfully execute the office of President of the United States, and will to the best of my ability, preserve, protect, and defend the Constitution of the United States."⁶⁰

Did Lincoln do as he promised? This question will be well answered, in his own words, in the following chapters.

SECESSION AND STATES' RIGHTS

WAS SECESSION LEGAL IN 1860? Of course! Since it is tacitly guaranteed in the Ninth and Tenth Amendments, since there is nothing in the U.S. Constitution prohibiting it, and since the U.S.A. was founded on the idea of secession, this important states' right has always been, and still is, perfectly legal—though Lincoln pretended it was not, just like his modern day Liberal descendants. And yet the destruction of secession was one of very reasons Lincoln took up arms against the South.[61]

What is almost impossible to grasp is that at one time Lincoln completely supported the idea of secession. Calling it a "most sacred right," here is what he had to say on the matter on January 12, 1848, in a speech before the U.S. House of Representatives, 12 years before he became president:

☞ "Any people anywhere, being inclined and having the power, have the right to rise up, and shake off the existing government, and form a new one that suits them better. This is a most valuable, a most sacred right—a right which, we hope and believe, is to liberate the world. Nor is this right confined to cases in which the whole people of an existing government may choose to exercise it. Any portion of such people that can may revolutionize, and make their own of so much of the territory as they inhabit."[62]

That same year, 1848, Lincoln backed Zachary Taylor for president, saying:
☞ "We prefer a candidate who, like General Taylor, will allow the people to have their own way regardless of private opinion; . . . he would force nothing on them which they don't want . . ."[63]

On October 16, 1854, during a speech at Peoria, Illinois, Lincoln said:
☞ "I trust I understand, and truly estimate the right of self-government. My faith in the proposition that each man should do precisely as he pleases with all which is exclusively his own, lies at the foundation of the sense of justice there is in me. I extend the principles to communities of men, as well as to individuals. I so extend it, because it is politically wise, as well as naturally just; politically wise, in saving us from broils about matters which do not concern us. Here, or at Washington, I would not trouble myself with the oyster laws of Virginia, or the cranberry laws of Indiana. . . . The doctrine of self government is right—absolutely and eternally right . . ."[64]

It is important to note here that antebellum Lincoln did not just support the idea of states' rights. During this same period he also publicly declared that he was a firm believer in the "principle of self-government," the political concept which formed the very foundation of the Southern Confederacy! He made one such pronouncement in a speech at Chicago, Illinois, on July 10, 1858. Refuting an accusation made by his political opponent Stephen A. Douglas, Lincoln said:
☞ "Now in relation to his inference that I am in favor of a general consolidation of all the local institutions of the various States. I will attend to that for a little while, and try to inquire, if I can, how on earth it could be that any man could draw such an inference from anything I said. I have said very many times in Judge Douglas's hearing that no man believed more than I in the principle of self-government; that it lies at the bottom of all my ideas of just government from beginning to end. . . . I think that I have said it in your hearing—that I believe each individual is naturally entitled to do as he pleases with himself and the fruit of his labor, so far as it in no wise interferes with any other man's rights; that each community, as a State, has a right to do exactly as it pleases with all the concerns within that State that interfere with the right of no other State; and that the General Government, upon principle, has no right to interfere with anything other than that general class of things that does concern the whole. I have said that at all times. I have said as illustrations that I do not believe in the right of Illinois to interfere with the cranberry laws of Indiana, the oyster laws of Virginia, or the liquor laws of Maine. I have said these things over and over again, and I repeat them here as my sentiments."[65]

On October 1, 1858, Lincoln wrote out this note for future speeches, showing that he not only understood the essential foundation of self-determination and states rights, but that he agreed with it as well:

☞ "I, too, believe in self-government as I understand it . . . I am for the people of the whole nation doing just as they please in all matters which concern the whole nation; for those of each part doing just as they choose in all matters which concern no other part; and for each individual doing just as he chooses in all matters which concern nobody else."[66]

At one time the lanky Liberal even cast himself as a Conservative Jeffersonian, as he writes in a letter dated April 6, 1859:

☞ ". . . it is now no child's play to save the principles of [Thomas] Jefferson from total overthrow in this nation. . . . The principles of Jefferson are the definitions and axioms of free society. And yet they are denied and evaded, with no small show of success. One dashingly calls them 'glittering generalities.' Another bluntly calls them 'self-evident lies.' And others insidiously argue that they apply to 'superior races.' These expressions, differing in form, are identical in object and effect—the supplanting the principles of free government, and restoring those of classification, caste, and legitimacy. They would delight a convocation of crowned heads plotting against the people. They are the vanguard, the miners and sappers of returning despotism. We must repulse them, or they will subjugate us. . . . All honor to Jefferson—to the man who, in the concrete pressure of a struggle for national independence by a single people, had the coolness, forecast, and capacity to introduce into a merely revolutionary document an abstract truth, applicable to all men and all times, and so to embalm it there that to-day and in all coming days it shall be a rebuke and a stumbling-block to the very harbingers of reappearing tyranny and oppression."[67]

As late as May 17, 1859, on which day he wrote the following in a letter to Dr. Theodore Canisius, he was defending states rights—at least in the North:

☞ "Dear Sir: Your note asking, in behalf of yourself and other German citizens, whether I am for or against the constitutional provision in regard to naturalized citizens, lately adopted by Massachusetts, and whether I am for or against a fusion of the Republicans, and other opposition elements, for the canvass of 1860, is received.

"Massachusetts is a sovereign and independent State; and it is no privilege of mine to scold her for what she does."⁶⁸

After winning his first presidential election, Lincoln continued to declare his support of states' rights, as he did in a December 28, 1860, letter to journalist, politician, and states' rights and free trade advocate Duff Green:

☞ "I declare that the maintenance inviolate of the rights of the States, and especially the right of each State to order and control its own domestic institutions according to its own judgment exclusively, is essential to that balance of powers on which the perfection and endurance of our political fabric depend; and I denounce the lawless invasion by armed force of the soil of any State or Territory, no matter under what pretext, as the gravest of crimes."⁶⁹

But then, a striking change occurred in the brain of our sixteenth chief executive. The penultimate demagogue, Lincoln always espoused whatever ideas would curry the most votes and win him financial backing. Thus, by the time he was in the White House, only a few months later, he found it politically expedient to denounce his party's Jeffersonian-like resolution concerning states' rights, while simultaneously declaring secession illegal, enabling him to plot his bloody and "lawless invasion by armed force" of the South. On March 4, 1861, during his First Inaugural Address, a fuming Lincoln began referring to secession as "the essence of anarchy":

☞ "That there are persons in one section or another who seek to destroy the Union at all events, and are glad of any pretext to do it, I will neither affirm nor deny; but if there be such, I need address no word to them. To those, however, who really love the Union may I not speak?

"Before entering upon so grave a matter as the destruction of our national fabric, with all its benefits, its memories, and its hopes, would it not be wise to ascertain precisely why we do it? Will you hazard so desperate a step while there is any possibility that any portion of the ills you fly from have no real existence? Will you, while the certain ills you fly to are greater than all the real ones you fly from—will you risk the commission of so fearful a mistake?

". . . If a minority in such case will secede rather than acquiesce, they make a precedent which in turn will divide and ruin them; for a minority of their own will secede from them whenever a majority refuses to be controlled by such minority. For instance, why may not any portion of a new confederacy a year or two hence arbitrarily secede again, precisely as portions of the present Union now claim to secede from it? All who cherish disunion sentiments are now being educated to the exact temper of doing this.

"Is there such perfect identity of interests among the States to compose a new Union, as to produce harmony only, and prevent renewed secession?

"Plainly, the central idea of secession is the essence of anarchy. A majority held in restraint by constitutional checks and limitations, and always changing easily with deliberate changes of popular opinions and sentiments, is the only true sovereign of a free people. Whoever rejects it does, of necessity, fly to anarchy or to despotism. Unanimity is impossible; the rule of a minority, as a permanent arrangement, is wholly inadmissible; so that, rejecting the majority principle, anarchy or despotism in some form is all that is left."[70]

More of Lincoln's garbled and irrational thoughts on secession soon followed, as, for instance, during his "Message to Congress in Special Session," delivered on July 4, 1861. Here, he refers to secession as a "sugar-coated" falsehood, a "farcical pretense," a "sophism" that has been "drugging the public mind for more than thirty years":

☞ "It might seem, at first thought, to be of little difference whether the present movement at the South be called 'secession' or 'rebellion.' The movers, however, well understand the difference. At the beginning they knew they could never raise their treason to any respectable magnitude by any name which implies violation of law. They knew their people possessed as much of moral sense, as much of devotion to law and order, and as much pride in and reverence for the history and government of their common country as any other civilized and patriotic people. They knew they could make no advancement directly in the teeth of these strong and, noble sentiments. Accordingly, they commenced by an insidious debauching of the public mind. They invented an ingenious sophism which, if conceded, was followed by perfectly logical steps, through all the incidents, to the complete destruction of the Union. The sophism itself is that any State of the Union may consistently with the National Constitution, and therefore lawfully and peacefully, withdraw from the Union without the consent of the Union or of any other State. The little disguise that the supposed right is to be exercised only for just cause, themselves to be the sole judges of its justice, is too thin to merit any notice.

"With rebellion thus sugar-coated they have been drugging the public mind of their section for more than thirty years, and until at length they have brought many good men to a willingness to take up arms against the government the day after some assemblage of men have enacted the farcical pretense of taking their State out of the Union, who could have been brought to no such thing the day before.

"This sophism derives much, perhaps the whole, of its currency from the assumption that there is some omnipotent and sacred supremacy pertaining to a State—to each State of our Federal Union."[71]

Certainly by the Autumn of 1863, Lincoln had apparently forgotten (or pretended to forget) his public statements from January 12, 1848, and July 10, 1858, in which he had thoroughly supported the legality of secession. For it was on November 9, 1863, that he lied, saying:

☞ "I have always thought the act of secession is legally nothing."[72]

Lincoln's main concern over the secession of the Southern states at this point was not slavery, or even the Confederacy's alleged desire to "destroy the Union," but rather with money, as he declared in the following three quotes from his July 4, 1861, "Message to Congress in Special Session":

☞ "What is now combated is the position that secession is consistent with the Constitution—is lawful and peaceful. It is not contended that there is any express law for it; and nothing should ever be implied as law which leads to unjust or absurd consequences. The nation purchased with money the countries out of which several of these States were formed. Is it just that they shall go off without leave and without refunding? The nation paid very large sums (in the aggregate, I believe, nearly a hundred millions) to relieve Florida of the aboriginal tribes. Is it just that she shall now be off without consent or without making any return? The nation is now in debt for money applied to the benefit of these so-called seceding States in common with the rest. Is it just either that creditors shall go unpaid or the remaining States pay the whole? A part of the present national debt was contracted to pay the old debts of Texas. Is it just that she shall leave and pay no part of this herself?"[73]

☞ "... if one State may secede, so may another; and when all have seceded, none is left to pay the debts. Is this quite just to creditors? Did we notify them of this sage view of ours when we borrowed their money? If we now recognize this doctrine by allowing the seceders to go in peace, it is difficult to see what we can do if others choose to go or to extort terms upon which they will promise to remain."[74]

☞ "The seceders insist that our Constitution admits of secession. They have assumed to make a national constitution of their own, in which of necessity they have either discarded or retained the right of secession as they insist it exists in ours. If they have discarded it, they thereby admit that on principle it ought not to be in ours. If they have retained it by their own construction of ours, they show that to be consistent they must secede from one another whenever they shall find it the easiest way of settling their debts, or effecting any other selfish or unjust object. The principle itself is one of disintegration, and upon which no government can possibly endure."[75]

Demagogic Lincoln was for states' rights before he became president, but against them afterward. Why? Political expediency.

THE UNION

PRESIDENT LINCOLN ARGUED AGAINST SECESSION using Daniel Webster's erroneous socialist theory that the Union was created before the states, and was thus superior to them in power and sovereignty.[76] In reality, not only did the states come before the Union and in fact create the Union, but the Union itself has no power over the states and no sovereignty unto itself, as the Ninth and Tenth Amendments of the U.S. Constitution intimate.[77] Still Lincoln held to his unsupportable theory, for he now had a political agenda: the complete destruction of states' rights so that he could install an all-powerful government in Washington, D.C., a Liberal, anti-American idea deceptively called the "American System"—one which we now refer to more accurately as "big government."[78]

Here, for example, is what he said during his July 4, 1861, "Message to Congress in Special Session":

☞ "Our States have neither more nor less power than that reserved to them in the Union by the Constitution—no one of them ever having been a State out of the Union. The original ones passed into the Union even before they cast off their British colonial dependence; and the new ones each came into the Union directly from condition of dependence, excepting Texas. And even Texas, in its temporary independence, was never designated a State. The new ones only took the designation of States on coming into the Union while that name was first adopted for the old ones in and by the Declaration of Independence. Therein the 'United Colonies' were declared to be 'free and independent States'; but even then the object plainly was not to declare their independence of one another or of the Union, but directly the contrary, as their mutual pledge and their mutual action before, at the time, and afterward, abundantly show. The express plighting of faith by each and all or the original thirteen in the Articles of Confederation, two years later, that the

Union shall be perpetual, is most conclusive. Having never been States either in substance or in name outside of the Union, whence this magical omnipotence of 'State Rights,' asserting a claim of power to lawfully destroy the Union itself? Much is said about the 'sovereignty' of the States; but the word even is not in the National Constitution, nor, as is believed, in any of the State constitutions. What is 'sovereignty' in the political sense of the term? Would it be far wrong to define it 'a political community without a political superior'? Tested by this, no one of our States except Texas ever was a sovereignty. And even Texas gave up the character on coming into the Union; by which act she acknowledged the Constitution of the United States, and the laws and treaties of the United States made in pursuance of the Constitution, to be for her the supreme law of the land. The States have their status in the Union, and they have no other legal status. If they break from this, they can only do so against law and by revolution. The Union, and not themselves separately, procured their independence and their liberty. By conquest or purchase the Union gave each of them whatever of independence or liberty it has. The Union is older than any of the States, and, in fact, it created them as States. Originally some dependent colonies made the Union, and, in turn, the Union threw off their old dependence for them, and made them States, such as they are. Not one of them ever had a State constitution independent of the Union. Of course, it is not forgotten that all the new States framed their constitutions before they entered the Union—nevertheless, dependent upon and preparatory to coming into the Union."[79]

Nearly every word of the above statement is incorrect, historically, legally, and politically. In 1866 pro-South advocate Edward A. Pollard wonderfully expressed the conservative South's reaction to this liberal nonsense:

> "In his message, Mr. Lincoln announced a great political discovery. It was that all former statesmen of America had lived, and written, and labored under a great delusion: that the States, instead of having created the Union, were its *creatures*; that they obtained their sovereignty and independence from it, and never possessed either until the [Constitutional] Convention of 1787. This singular doctrine of consolidation was the natural preface to a series of measures to strengthen the Government, to enlarge the Executive power, and to conduct the war with new decision, and on a most unexpected scale of magnitude."[80]

Like many other 19th-Century Northerners, Liberal Lincoln espoused numerous historically inaccurate and even wildly un-American views about our country and its government, none that you will ever read about in pro-North versions of the Civil War. Among them were his beliefs that the Union existed before the states, that whites are superior to other races, that the president can interpret the Constitution however he sees fit, that the Southern states should be identical to the Northern ones, that there are no such things as states' rights, and that the U.S. was meant only for Caucasians. The vast majority of Victorian Southerners, of course, repudiated such views.

THE CAUSE AND PURPOSE OF THE WAR

ACCORDING TO PRO-NORTH HISTORIANS AND scholars, the American "Civil War"[81] was fought over slavery.[82] However, the words of Lincoln—the man who started the conflict—prove otherwise, as this revealing chapter illustrates.

During his First Inaugural Address on March 4, 1861, Lincoln stated the following clearly and unequivocally, proving for all who care to listen, that slavery was not the cause of the Civil War—which began a mere month later on April 12:

☞ "Apprehension seems to exist among the people of the Southern States that by the accession of a Republican administration their property and their peace and personal security are to be endangered. There has never been any reasonable cause for such apprehension. Indeed, the most ample evidence to the contrary has all the while existed and been open to their inspection. It is found in nearly all the published speeches of him who now addresses you. I do but quote from one of those speeches when I declare that 'I have no purpose, directly or indirectly, to interfere with the institution of slavery in the States where it exists. I believe I have no lawful right to do so, and I have no inclination to do so.' Those who nominated and elected me did so with full knowledge that I had made this and many similar declarations and had never recanted them."[83]

Such statements matched those he made long before becoming president, such as this note he made on October 1, 1858, for an upcoming speech:

☞ "The idea of forcing slavery into a free State, or out of a slave State, at the point of the bayonet, is alike nonsensical. Slavery can only become extinct by being restricted to its present limits, and dwindling out."[84]

From the same set of notes comes this statement:

☞ "To give the victory to the right [that is, the antislavery faction], not bloody bullets, but peaceful ballots only are necessary. Thanks to our good old Constitution, and organization under it, these alone are necessary. It only needs that every right thinking man shall go to the polls, and without fear or prejudice vote as he thinks."[85]

Several years into his War, on April 18, 1864, during a speech at a "Sanitary Fair" in Baltimore, Maryland, Lincoln expresses surprise that slavery had even been dragged into the conflict. This was over a year after he had issued his Final Emancipation Proclamation:

☞ "When the war began, three years ago, neither party, nor any man, expected it would last till now. . . . Neither did any anticipate that domestic slavery would be much affected by the war."[86]

As late as February 13, 1865, just two months before he died, Lincoln tells his commanding officers in West Tennessee that:

☞ ". . . the object of the war being to restore and maintain the blessings of peace and good government, I desire you to help, and not hinder, every advance in that direction."[87]

In an unfinished letter to Isaac M. Schermerhorn, dated September 12, 1864, Lincoln writes:

☞ "The preservation of our Union was not the sole avowed object for which the war was commenced. It was commenced for precisely the reverse object—to destroy our Union. . . . It is true, however, that the administration accepted the war thus commenced for the sole avowed object of preserving our Union; and it is not true that it has since been, or will be, prosecuted by this administration for any other object. In declaring this I only declare what I can know and do know to be true, and what no other man can know to be false."⁸⁸

On August 15, 1864, only eight months before the end of the Civil War, Lincoln gave what is without question the most definitive and explicit statement regarding its cause. Once again, according to our sixteenth president, it was not slavery:

☞ "My enemies pretend I am now carrying on this war for the sole purpose of abolition. So long as I am President, it shall be carried on for the sole purpose of restoring the Union. . . . Let my enemies prove to the country that the destruction of slavery is not necessary to a restoration of the Union. I will abide the issue."⁸⁹

What has confused many is the following statement, which Lincoln made during his December 1, 1862, "Annual Message to Congress." Often used by Lincolnites to "prove" that the War was over slavery, it is not at all what is commonly thought. Double-talk, contradiction, and obfuscation were hallmarks of Lincoln's duplicitous tactics to confuse his enemies and try to maintain the support of abolitionists, as this quote aptly demonstrates:

☞ "Without slavery the rebellion could never have existed; without slavery it could not continue."⁹⁰

Adding to the confusion caused by Lincoln's many contradictory remarks are the following words from his Second Inaugural Address, given March 4, 1865. Despite what he says here, all educated people knew then and know now that it is more than evident that slavery was neither the "cause" or the "strength" of the Confederacy. This statement is just more Lincolnian disinformation, meant to baffle his critics, whip up anti-South support in the North, raise money, curry votes, and agitate the South. Four years ago, the president says disingenuously:

☞ "One-eighth of the whole population were colored slaves, not distributed generally over the Union, but localized in the Southern part of it. These slaves constituted a peculiar and powerful interest. All knew that this interest was, somehow, the cause of the war. To strengthen, perpetuate, and extend this interest was the object for which the insurgents would rend the Union, even by war; while the government claimed no right to do more than to restrict the territorial enlargement of it."⁹¹

When confronted as to why he made such conflicting statements to the public, Lincoln gave away the secret behind his modus operandi with the following sensational and revealing remark:
☞ "My policy is to have no policy."⁹²

One of the real causes of Lincoln's War was surely his numerous anti-South, highly inflammatory public declarations, such as this one from a June 16, 1858, speech at Springfield, Illinois, which was purposefully designed to provoke Southerners:
☞ "'A house divided against itself cannot stand.' I believe this government cannot endure permanently half slave and half free. . . . It will become all one thing, or all the other."⁹³

For big spending, big government Lincoln, few things were more important than money and his left-wing goal of totally controlling the U.S. treasury and economy. Indeed, Lincoln's obscene obsession with "tariffs," "duties," and "revenue" turns out to be the foundation of his attempt to subjugate the South, for money is at the root of all wars, is it not? Consider a meeting that Confederate Colonel John Brown Baldwin had with Lincoln shortly after he became president. It was at this time (early 1861) that Baldwin traveled from Virginia to the White House to meet with the new chief executive to confer upon the War. Why can the North not allow the South to go in peace? the Colonel asked, to which Lincoln replied:
☞ "If I let the South go on what will become of my tariff?"⁹⁴

Lincoln had a similar conversation with Confederate official Alexander H. Stuart. Just prior to the War several Confederate peace commissioners, including Stuart, had an interview with the newly sworn in Yankee president in an attempt to avoid the coming bloodbath. At the meeting Stuart pleaded for time and further discussions, to which Lincoln replied impatiently:

☞ "If I do that [that is, recognize the Southern Confederacy], what will become of my revenue? I might as well shut up housekeeping at once."[95]

Also revealing is Lincoln's statement to William Kellogg on June 29, 1863:
☞ "Profit controls all."[96]

While he continued to fuss and fume over the potential massive loss of "revenue" if the Southern states were allowed to permanently secede, Lincoln maintained that the real and only reason he was waging war on the South was to "preserve the Union," a lie he kept up until his final days. On April 11, 1865, during his last public address, for instance, he mentions slavery only once, but goes into great detail about the rebellion and secession. In fact, he states quite clearly that the "sole object" of the entire conflict was bringing the Confederate states back into the United States:
☞ "We all agree that the seceded States, so called, are out of their proper practical relation with the Union, and that the sole object of the government, civil and military, in regard to those States is to again get them into that proper practical relation."[97]

This was no last minute statement, meant to fool the public into thinking that his War was really not about abolishing slavery. Over a year earlier, on June 16, 1864, at a "Sanitary Fair" in Philadelphia, Pennsylvania, Lincoln said:
☞ "We accepted this war for an object, a worthy object, and the war will end when that object is attained. Under God, I hope it never will end until that time. Speaking of the present campaign, General [Ulysses S.] Grant is reported to have said, 'I am going through on this line if it takes all summer.' This war has taken three years; it was begun or accepted upon the line of restoring the national authority over the whole national domain, and for the American people, as far as my knowledge enables me to speak, I say we are going through on this line if it takes three years more."[98]

So what was the real cause of the "Civil War"? Lincoln, along with the U.S. Congress, repeatedly said that the North fought only to "preserve the Union," while his Southern opponent, President Jefferson Davis, repeatedly said the South fought only to preserve political self-determination—the core idea of the Founding Fathers.⁹⁹ If there are any doubts left in the minds of my readers, consider this final quote, made by Lincoln in the summer of 1861. After angrily revoking an attempt by one of his officers to emancipate slaves in Missouri (just one of the many times he did this), the Yankee president had a conversation with abolitionist Reverend Charles Edward Lester. Lincoln expressed his impatience with Lester and other Northern abolitionists who were pushing for emancipation. Said Lincoln:

☞ "I think [Massachusetts Senator Charles] Sumner, and the rest of you, would upset our apple-cart altogether, if you had your way. . . . We didn't go into the war to put down Slavery, but to put the flag back, and to act differently at this moment, would, I have no doubt, not only weaken our cause, but smack of bad faith; for I never should have had votes enough to send me here, if the people had supposed I should try to use my power to upset Slavery. Why, the first thing you'd see, would be a mutiny in the army. No! We must wait until every other means has been exhausted. This thunderbolt will keep."¹⁰⁰

Lincoln has been called "America's greatest abolitionist." But his own words and actions tell a different story.

If Lincoln believed, as he states in the following September 15, 1858, remark, that slavery was about to come to an end naturally (which is what the South believed as well), why wage a major war over it? The very idea is irrational in the extreme:

☞ "I say, in the way our fathers originally left the slavery question, the institution was in the course of ultimate extinction, and the public mind rested in the belief that it was in the course of ultimate extinction."¹⁰¹

---

*Those who continue to believe that the Civil War was fought over slavery must ask themselves why, if this is true, did the conflict continue for another two years after Lincoln issued the Emancipation Proclamation on January 1, 1863? If Lincoln's War had been about ending slavery, both sides would have laid down their arms that day.*¹⁰²

ABOLITION

THOUGH WE HAVE BEEN TAUGHT that Lincoln was an abolitionist, he was anything but, as this chapter will show. True abolitionists wanted to end slavery then fully incorporate blacks into American society as equal citizens with full civil rights. Lincoln did not come close to fitting into this category. He was actually what would be most accurately called an emancipationist-colonizationist.

While he did eventually decide that he wanted to restrict then end slavery, it was not because the human rights of blacks were being violated. It was because he was a white separatist who preferred living in a white-only America, a goal he was hoping to achieve through colonization; that is, deporting blacks out of the country and resettling them in foreign colonies.

The problem for Lincoln was that he could not do this as long as blacks were enslaved, for under the Constitution slaves were considered the "private property" of their owners.[103]

For Lincoln then, emancipating the slaves would kill two birds with one stone: abolition would remove what he considered the "dangerous" presence of blacks from white homes, farms, and towns,[104] while at the same time allowing him to legally colonize freed blacks outside of the country, preferably, as he often said, so he could ship them "back to their native land," Africa.[105]

When asked once how he felt about having abolitionists in his political party, Lincoln impatiently replied:
☞ "As long as I'm not tarred with the abolitionist brush."[106]

If Lincoln was truly the "Great Emancipator," as Northern myth asserts, one would think that the first item on his agenda as president would have been to abolish slavery in our nation's capital city, Washington, D.C. Instead, he stalled and deferred month after month, until over a year passed. As President-elect Lincoln said on December 15, 1860, just a few months prior to his inauguration:

☞ "I have no thought of recommending the abolition of slavery in the District of Columbia, nor the slave-trade among the slave States."[107]

Once compared to the crucified Christ by men like New Englander Henry David Thoreau,[108] *Yankee abolitionist and psychopathic murderer John Brown is still considered a hero by many uninformed Yankees and New South Southerners. Yet here, on February 9, 1860, is what Lincoln had to say about the madman's illegal and futile attempt to free Southern slaves and launch slave riots across Dixie:*

☞ "John Brown's effort was peculiar. It was not a slave insurrection. It was an attempt by white men to get up a revolt among slaves, in which the slaves refused to participate. In fact, it was so absurd that the slaves, with all their ignorance, saw plainly enough it could not succeed."[109]

Lincoln was so far from being an abolitionist that he often blocked the freeing of slaves, such as when he countermanded the emancipation proclamations of his cabinet members and military officers, including Simon Cameron,[110] *John W. Phelps,*[111] *John C. Frémont,*[112] *Jim Lane,*[113] *and David Hunter*[114]—*proving once and for all, if nothing else does, that Lincoln did not wage war against the South over slavery.*[115] *Here, from May 17, 1862, for example, is Lincoln's brief order to Union General Hunter to cease freeing slaves:*

☞ "No commanding general shall do such a thing upon my responsibility without consulting me."[116]

Two days later, on March 19, Lincoln made his countermand official by issuing a "Proclamation Revoking General Hunter's Order Of Military Emancipation." In it the anti-abolition president clearly states that he will only emancipate the slaves when and if it becomes "a necessity indispensable to the maintenance of the government":

☞ "By The President Of The United States Of America: A Proclamation.

"Whereas there appears in the public prints what purports to be a proclamation of Major-General Hunter . . . I, Abraham Lincoln, President of the United States, proclaim and declare that . . . whether it be competent for me, as commander-in-chief of the army and navy, to declare the slaves of any State or States free, and whether, at any time, in any case, it shall have become a necessity indispensable to the maintenance of the government to exercise such supposed power, are questions which, under my responsibility, I reserve to myself, and which I cannot feel justified in leaving to the decision of commanders in the field."[117]

When Union General John Frémont issued his own emancipation proclamation, Lincoln sent him an angry letter on September 2, 1861, noting that liberating slaves would interfere with his political goal to force Kentucky to stay in the Union:

☞ "I think there is great danger that . . . the confiscation of property and the liberating slaves of traitorous owners, will alarm our Southern Union friends and turn them against us; perhaps ruin our rather fair prospect for Kentucky."[118]

Lincoln's anti-abolition activities did not go unnoticed by his few slavery-hating constituents. One of these was Illinois Senator Orville Hickman Browning, one of the president's oldest friends. When a shocked Browning sent a letter to Lincoln questioning his countermand of Frémont's emancipation proclamation, he received this sharp response on September 22, 1861:

☞ "(Private and Confidential.) Executive Mansion, Washington. Hon. O. H. Browning. My dear Sir: Yours of the 17th is just received: and coming from you, I confess it astonishes me. . . . General Fremont's proclamation as to confiscation of property and the liberation of slaves is purely political and not within the range of military law or necessity."[119]

Despite such obvious anti-abolitionist activities as the Frémont debacle (the slavery-hating Union officer was later relieved of his command), to this day Lincoln's devoted followers continue to insist that the president was an abolitionist. Yet if he was, we must wonder why he made the following public statement on October 15, 1858, at Alton, Illinois:

☞ "It is nothing but a miserable perversion of what I have said, to assume that I have declared Missouri, or any other Slave State, shall emancipate her slaves; I have proposed no such thing."[120]

Two years later, Lincoln ran for president on a party platform that called for upholding slavery in the South. His nomination in 1860 by fellow party members was, after all, due to the fact that as a white supremacist he was considered a "safe" candidate,[121] *a trait for which he had a long and distinguished history. As early as 1837, for example, while he was still a young member of his state's legislature, Lincoln made it a practice to send anti-abolition statements to the U.S. House of Representatives, as he did on March 3 under the title "Protest in the Illinois Legislature on the Subject of Slavery." Here, an obviously irritated Lincoln wrote that when it comes to slavery,*

☞ "the promulgation of abolition doctrines tends rather to increase than abate its evils."[122]

I do not see, Lincoln warned members of the Springfield, Illinois, State House on July 16, 1852,

☞ "how it [slavery] could be at once eradicated without producing a greater evil even to the cause of liberty itself."[123]

On September 15, 1858, Lincoln told his audience at Jonesboro, Illinois, that the Whig (Liberal) party did not get a "good name" until it was dissolved (after which it was replaced by the Republican party—created by Liberals and socialists in 1854)[124] *and the public stopped associating it with "abolitionism":*

☞ "I recollect in the presidential election which followed, when we had General [Winfield] Scott up for the presidency; Judge [Stephen A.] Douglas was around berating us Whigs as Abolitionists, precisely as he does to-day—not a bit of difference. I have often heard him. We could do nothing when the Old Whig party was alive that was not Abolitionism, but it has got an extremely good name since it has passed away."[125]

Naturally, Lincoln was heartily despised by abolitionists, who, from the very first day of his presidency, were extremely annoyed with him. Why? Because he had not yet called for the immediate destruction of slavery. Toward the end of 1862, for instance, two years into his first term, antislavery leaders and organizations continued to express their unhappiness with Lincoln over his reluctance, even his refusal, to emancipate the nation's slaves.[126] *In June 1863, six months* after *issuing his Final Emancipation Proclamation, Lincoln was still offering to protect slave owners.*[127] *It was just such efforts to defend slavers, stall black enlistment, and hinder abolition that earned him the nickname the "tortoise President" from fellow Yankees.*[128] *An example: on July 4, 1863, a laconic Lincoln wrote the following to Yankee General Robert Cumming Schenck concerning freeing then enlisting blacks in the Union army:*

☞ "Your despatches about negro regiments are not uninteresting or unnoticed by us, but we have not been quite ready to respond. . ."[129]

Lincoln once made note of the extreme pressure he was constantly under to issue an emancipation proclamation. This particular instance occurred on July 12, 1862, when, obviously uncomfortable, he begged representatives of the Border States to consider his favored plan: gradual-compensated emancipation and the subsequent deportation of freed blacks. He begins by making reference to his countermand of one of his officers' own personal emancipation proclamations:

☞ "I am pressed with a difficulty not yet mentioned—one which threatens division among those who, united, are none too strong. An instance of it is known to you. General [David] Hunter is an honest man. He was, and I hope still is, my friend. I valued him none the less for his agreeing with me in the general wish that all men everywhere could be free. He proclaimed all men free within certain States, and I repudiated the proclamation. He expected more good and less harm from the measure than I could believe would follow. Yet, in repudiating it, I gave dissatisfaction, if not offense, to many whose support the country cannot afford to lose. And this is not the end of it. The pressure in this direction is still upon me, and is increasing. By conceding what I now ask, you can relieve me, and, much more, can relieve the country, in this important point."[130]

In a December 29, 1862, letter to John Alexander McClernand, Lincoln admits that he has purposefully delayed emancipation:

☞ "After the commencement of hostilities, I struggled nearly a year and a half to get along without touching the 'institution'; and when finally I conditionally determined to touch it, I gave a hundred days' fair notice of my purpose to all the States and people, within which time they could have turned it wholly aside by simply again becoming good citizens of the United States."[131]

That Lincoln did not consider himself an abolitionist, that he in fact intentionally delineated himself from them, is clearly evidenced by numerous statements he made. One of the earliest of these occurred in a October 3, 1845, letter where he referred to "the liberty men,"[132] a 19th-Century term for abolitionists. If Lincoln had considered himself one of them he would have said "we Liberty men." In the same letter he says:

☞ "If the . . . abolitionists had voted with us last fall, [Liberal] Mr. [Henry] Clay would now be President . . ."[133]

Lincoln made a similar statement during one of his debates with Illinois Senator Stephen A. Douglas, this one at Chicago on July 10, 1858:

☞ "I have always hated slavery, I think, as much as any Abolitionist."[134]

"Anti-slavery man" Lincoln, as he called himself,[135] did not come close to meeting the criteria of being an authentic abolitionist (that is, one who supported both emancipation and *full civil and equal rights for blacks*). Just two years before he became president he asserted that he did not even care if abolition ever took place. Here is what he said during the same July 10 debate at Chicago, where he was accused of espousing abolitionist sentiment:

☞ "[Senator Douglas] says that I am in favor of making war by the North upon the South for the extinction of slavery; that I am also in favor of inviting (as he expresses it) the South to a war upon the North, for the purpose of nationalizing slavery. Now, it is singular enough, if you will carefully read that passage over, that I did not say that I was in favor of anything in it. I only said what I expected would take place. I made a prediction only—it may have been a foolish one, perhaps. I did not even say that I desired that slavery should be put in course of ultimate extinction."[136]

At the same debate Lincoln went on to make the following remark:

☞ "I have said a hundred times, and I have now no inclination to take it back, that I believe there is no right and ought to be no inclination in the people of the free States to enter into the slave States and interfere with the question of slavery at all."[137]

On September 17, 1859, Lincoln made a similar comment. After my party wins at the polls in 1860, he told an audience made up primarily of Kentuckians:
☞ "We mean to leave you alone, and in no way to interfere with your institution; to abide by all and every compromise of the Constitution . . ."[138]

Far earlier, on March 3, 1837, Lincoln, along with Dan Stone, sent a "protest" to the Illinois legislature "on the subject of slavery." It reads:
☞ "Resolutions upon the subject of domestic slavery having passed both branches of the General Assembly at its present session, the undersigned hereby protest against the passage of the same.

"They believe that the institution of slavery is founded on both injustice and bad policy, but that the promulgation of abolition doctrines tends rather to increase than abate its evils.

"They believe that the Congress of the United States has no power under the Constitution to interfere with the institution of slavery in the different States.

"They believe that the Congress of the United States has the power, under the Constitution, to abolish slavery in the District of Columbia, but that the power ought not to be exercised, unless at the request of the people of the District.

"The difference between these opinions and those contained in the said resolutions is their reason for entering this protest."[139]

If Lincoln was a true abolitionist, as pro-North historians tell us, we must ask ourselves several questions. Why did he, at first, continually promise not to interfere with the institution?[140] Why, as an attorney, did he defend, not slaves, but slave owners?[141] Why did he use slave labor instead of free labor to construct the White House, the Capitol, and other Federal buildings and roads in Washington, D.C.?[142] Why did it take until April 16, 1862, for the passage of the District of Columbia Emancipation Act, which, while abolishing slavery in Washington,[143] also called for the deportation of freed blacks?[144] If he was truly an abolitionist, one would think that the first item on his agenda as president would have been to abolish slavery in America's capital city. Instead, he stalled and deferred month after month, until over a year passed. As he said in a public speech at Freeport, Illinois, on August 27, 1858, a mere one and half years

before entering the White House:
☛ "I do not stand to-day pledged to the abolition of slavery in the District of Columbia."¹⁴⁵

More importantly, as the president-elect said on December 15, 1860, just a few months prior to his inauguration:
☛ "I have no thought of recommending the abolition of slavery in the District of Columbia, nor the slave-trade among the slave States."¹⁴⁶

---

*On his way from Springfield, Illinois, to his inauguration in Washington, D.C., Lincoln paused on February 27, 1861, to write a quick reply to the city's mayor, James Gabriel Berret, about his concerns of slavery being abolished there.*¹⁴⁷ *Lincoln tacitly assures Berret that under his presidency he would not allow this to happen:*
☛ "Mr. Mayor: I thank you, and through you the municipal authorities of this city who accompany you, for this welcome. And as it is the first time in my life, since the present phase of politics has presented itself in this country, that I have said anything publicly within a region of country where the institution of slavery exists, I will take this occasion to say that I think very much of the ill feeling that has existed and still exists between the people in the section from which I came [Illinois] and the people here, is dependent upon a misunderstanding of one another. I therefore avail myself of this opportunity to assure you, Mr. Mayor, and all the gentlemen present, that I have not now, and never have had, any other than as kindly feelings toward you as to the people of my own section. I have not now, and never have had, any disposition to treat you in any respect otherwise than as my own neighbors. I have not now any purpose to withhold from you any of the benefits of the Constitution, under any circumstances, that I would not feel myself constrained to withhold from my own neighbors; and I hope, in a word, that when we shall become better acquainted—and I say it with great confidence—we shall like each other better. I thank you for the kindness of this reception."¹⁴⁸

If Lincoln was a real abolitionist why did he delay issuing the Final Emancipation Proclamation for even longer, until January 1, 1863, two years into his presidency?

Why did he at first prohibit blacks (along with Native-Americans) from serving in the U.S. military?[149] *And why did he bar free blacks from entering the White House?*[150] *The answer is that he was not a true abolitionist, for he did not want freed slaves to receive full civil rights or live in close proximity to Northern whites. In fact, he did not even want them to live in the U.S. after emancipation. His goal was always to end slavery, free blacks, and "ship them," as he so indelicately put it, "back to Africa." Abolition first, deportation second, this was always Lincoln's stated goal. Little wonder that Northern abolitionists, like Liberal Charles Sumner, referred to Lincoln as "America's largest slave owner."*[151] *Here, at Peoria, Illinois, on October 16, 1854, is how our colonizationist president described his real feelings on slavery, abolition, and American blacks:*

☞ "If all earthly power were given me, I should not know what to do as to the existing institution. My first impulse would be to free all the slaves, and send them to Liberia [Africa]—to their own native land. But a moment's reflection would convince me, that whatever of high hope (as I think there is) there may be in this, in the long run, its sudden execution is impossible. If they were all landed there in a day, they would all perish in the next ten days; and there are not surplus shipping and surplus money enough in the world to carry them there in many times ten days. What then? Free them all, and keep them among us as underlings? Is it quite certain that this betters their condition? I think I would not hold one in slavery at any rate; yet the point is not clear enough to me to denounce people upon. What next? Free them, and make them politically and socially our equals? My own feelings will not admit of this; and if mine would, we well know that those of the great mass of white people will not."[152]

After the New York Draft Riots, July 12 to July 16, 1863, in which hundreds of innocent blacks had been viciously and mindlessly murdered by racist white Northerners, Lincoln responded in his usual apathetic way: no comment. Even when he was advised to appoint a commission to conduct an inquiry into the horrendous incident, he stonily refused, saying:

☞ "Better let the dirt alone,—at least for the present. One rebellion at a time is about as much as we can conveniently handle."[153]

Lincoln's lackadaisical attitude toward blacks and slavery was evident from the fact that he considered himself a member of a group that he carefully defined as,

☞ "those for it [the Union] with or without [slavery], but prefer it without."[154]

In his reply to Senator Stephen A. Douglas during their August 27, 1858, debate at Freeport, Illinois, an obviously perturbed Lincoln assures his opponent, yet again, that he is not an abolitionist:

☞ "The judge has again addressed himself to the Abolition tendencies of a speech of mine, made at Springfield in June last. I have so often tried to answer what he is always saying on that melancholy theme, that I almost turn with disgust from the discussion—from the repetition of an answer to it. I trust that nearly all of this intelligent audience have read that speech. If you have, I may venture to leave it to you to inspect it closely, and see whether it contains any of those 'bugaboos' which frighten Judge Douglas."[155]

Mary Todd, Lincoln's wife, testified to the fact that her husband was completely nonreligious, refused to attend church, and never once cracked open the Good Book.

SLAVERY

WHEN IT CAME TO SLAVERY, Lincoln focused all his attention on the South. But he need not have, for not only was the American abolition movement born in Dixie[156] (Virginia was the first state to prohibit slavery),[157] but in 1860 only 4.8 percent of the Southern populace owned slaves.[158]

Clearly, slavery was far from being the "cornerstone" of Southern society.[159] Indeed, it was detested by nearly all Southerners, even most slave owners, and it was their hope and prayer that the institution would die out as soon as possible—as Robert E. Lee, Mary Chesnut, Patrick R. Cleburne, and thousands of other prominent Southerners repeatedly declared.[160]

Anti-South proponents do not want you to know these facts, but ever since America's first voluntary emancipation in *Virginia* in 1655[161] (Southerner Thomas Jefferson tried to end slavery in the 1700s),[162] Southerners had been pushing for abolition, looking forward to slavery's imminent extinction.[163]

The fact is that Lincoln should have been targeting his sights not on the South, but on the North, the region where both the American slave trade was born (in Massachusetts in 1638)[164] and where American slavery got its start (in Massachusetts in 1641).[165] Though there were many others across the Northeast, the earliest and largest slave centers in the U.S. were Boston, Massachusetts; Providence, Rhode Island; Baltimore, Maryland; Philadelphia, Pennsylvania; and above all New York City, New York.[166]

The South, on the other hand, had no slave centers. Why? Because the South never traded in slaves, and in fact banned the practice (in the Confederate Constitution) four years before the North did.[167] The only slave ships to sail from the U.S. to Africa all sailed from Northern ports.[168] All flew the U.S. flag, all were commandeered by Yankee captains, all were funded by Yankee money, all unloaded their human cargo in Yankee cities—after which they were sold south.[169]

Just as American slavery has been completely misrepresented by pro-North historians,[170] so too has Lincoln's attitude toward the institution. The truth, from his own mouth, is that he was not an abolitionist and he was not particularly against slavery itself. As he said time and time again, he was mainly against the spread of slavery outside the South. Why?

Because he did not want blacks, enslaved or free, to intermarry or even intermingle with Northern and Western whites, or have to compete with them over land, homes, and jobs. Later, when he realized that he could not stop the expansion of the institution, he decided that emancipating blacks then deporting them back to Africa was the best policy, as we will see in Chapter 13. Let us now examine Lincoln's words concerning his actual feelings toward slavery.

As evidence that it was the North who traded in slaves, not the South, we have the case of Captain Nathaniel Gordon of New York, the only person ever tried, convicted, and executed for slaving: on February 21, 1862, he was put to death by Lincoln's personal order.[171] *In the following February 4th missive, Lincoln grants Gordon a temporary stay of execution:*

☞ "Whereas it appears that at a term of the Circuit Court of the United States of America for the southern district of New York, held in the month of November, A. D. 1861, Nathaniel Gordon was indicted and convicted for being engaged in the slave-trade, and was by the said court sentenced to be put to death by hanging by the neck on Friday the 7th day of February, A. D. 1862;

"And whereas a large number of respectable citizens have earnestly besought me to commute the said sentence of the said Nathaniel Gordon to a term of imprisonment for life, which application I have felt it to be my duty to refuse;

"And whereas it has seemed to me probable that the unsuccessful application made for the commutation of his sentence may have prevented the said Nathaniel Gordon from making the necessary preparation for the awful change which awaits him:

"Now, therefore, be it known that I, Abraham Lincoln, President of the United States of America, have granted and do hereby grant unto him, the said Nathaniel Gordon, a respite of the above-recited sentence until Friday, the 21st day of February, A. D. 1862, between the hours of twelve o'clock at noon and three o'clock in the afternoon of the said day, when the said sentence shall be executed.

"In granting this respite it becomes my painful duty to admonish the prisoner that, relinquishing all expectation of pardon by human authority, he refer himself alone to the mercy of the common God and Father of all men."[172]

More evidence of the Northern slave trade comes from the fact that the last American slave ship to be captured by the U.S. government was a Northern one: the Nightingale, also from New York, confiscated on April 21, 1861. At the time of its seizure, this vessel, from the so-called "abolitionist North," had nearly 1,000 manacled Africans on board.[173] It was doing "business as usual" up until the first few weeks of the "Civil War."[174] Lincoln refers to Captain Gordon, along with the Nightingale and several other seized Yankee slave ships, in his First Annual Message to Congress on December 3, 1861:

☞ "The execution of the laws for the suppression of the African slave-trade has been confided to the Department of the Interior. It is a subject of gratulation that the efforts which have been made for the suppression of this inhuman traffic have been recently attended with unusual success. Five vessels being fitted out for the slave-trade have been seized and condemned. Two mates of vessels engaged in the trade, and one person in equipping a vessel as a slaver, have been convicted and subjected to the penalty of fine and imprisonment, and one captain, taken with a cargo of Africans on board his vessel, has been convicted of the highest grade of offense under our laws, the punishment of which is death."[175]

Before he became U.S. president, Lincoln (a former Southerner) was perfectly aware that the majority of Southerners were against slavery and wanted nothing more than to rid themselves of the institution. Yet, after he entered the White House in 1861 it now suited his purpose better to claim the opposite; namely, that the South's sole ambition was to maintain and spread slavery throughout the U.S. Here, in an October 16, 1854, speech, is what Lincoln said seven years prior to becoming president:

☞ "How common is the remark now in the slave States, 'If we were only clear of our slaves, how much better it would be for us.'"[176]

One year before being elected president Lincoln was adamant that he had no interest in interfering with slavery, as he noted in a September 17, 1859, speech at Cincinnati,

Ohio:
☞ "[I said at an earlier date that] I believe we have no power, under the Constitution of the United States, or rather under the form of government under which we live, to interfere with the institution of slavery, or any other of the institutions of our sister States, be they free or slave States. I declared then, and I now re-declare, that I have as little inclination to interfere with the institution of slavery where it now exists, through the instrumentality of the General Government, or any other instrumentality, as I believe we have no power to do so."[177]

On September 17, 1859, at Columbus, Ohio, Lincoln told the Southerners in his audience:
☞ "I will tell you, so far as I am authorized to speak for the opposition, what we mean to do with you. . . . We mean to leave you alone, and in no way to interfere with your institution [of slavery]; to abide by all and every compromise of the Constitution . . ."[178]

Just over two years before he was elected president, during a speech at Chicago, Illinois, on July 10, 1858 (in which he replied to charges made by his senatorial opponent Stephen A. Douglas), Lincoln made these remarks:
☞ "I have said that always; Judge Douglas has heard me say it—if not quite a hundred times, at least as good as a hundred times; and when it is said that I am in favor of interfering with slavery where it exists, I know it is unwarranted by anything I have ever intended, and, as I believe, by anything I have ever said. If by any means I have ever used language which could fairly be so construed (as, however, I believe I never have), I now correct it.

"So much, then, for the inference that Judge Douglas draws, that I am in favor of setting the sections at war with one another. I know that I never meant any such thing, and I believe that no fair mind can infer any such thing from anything I have ever said."[179]

During his second debate with Douglas on August 27, 1858, at Freeport, Illinois, Lincoln used the occasion to clarify and emphasize his positions on the various aspects of slavery, including what he would come to call one of his primary goals, "the

preventing of the spread and nationalization of slavery."[180] *Lincoln begins by replying to a series of Douglas' questions concerning slavery:*
☞ "I do not now, nor ever did, stand in favor of the unconditional repeal of the fugitive-slave law. [Note: This constitutional law (Article 4, Section 2, Clause 3) required slaves to be returned to their owners.][181]

". . . I do not now, nor ever did, stand pledged against the admission of any more slave States into the Union.

". . . I do not stand to-day pledged to the abolition of slavery in the District of Columbia.

". . . I do not stand pledged to the prohibition of the slave-trade between the different States.

". . . I am not generally opposed to honest acquisition of territory [with or without slavery first being prohibited therein]; and, in any given case, I would or would not oppose such acquisition, accordingly as I might think such acquisition would or would not aggravate the slavery question among ourselves."[182]

In the same speech Lincoln elaborates on his opinion of the fugitive slave law:
☞ ". . . in regard to the fugitive-slave law, I have never hesitated to say, and I do not now hesitate to say, that I think, under the Constitution of the United States, the people of the Southern States are entitled to a congressional fugitive-slave law."[183]

On December 11, 1860, President-elect Lincoln made the following comment in a letter to William Kellogg:
☞ "You know I think the fugitive-slave clause of the Constitution ought to be enforced—to put it in its mildest form, ought not to be resisted."[184]

Two months later, on February 1, 1861, just one month before he was inaugurated, Lincoln shared his thoughts regarding both the American slave trade and the fugitive slave issue with his future secretary of state Yankee Liberal William H. Seward:
☞ "As to fugitive slaves, . . . slave-trade among the slave States, and whatever springs of necessity from the fact that the institution is amongst us, I care but little . . ."[185]

From an August 27, 1858, speech, at Freeport, Illinois:
☞ "In regard to . . . whether I am pledged to the admission of any more slave States into the Union, I state to you very frankly that . . . if slavery shall be kept out of the Territories during the territorial existence of any one given Territory, and then the people shall, having a fair chance and a clear field, when they come to adopt the Constitution, do such an extraordinary thing as to adopt a slave constitution, uninfluenced by the actual presence of the institution among them, I see no alternative, if we own the country, but to admit them into the Union."[186]

Lincoln was against freeing the slaves in Washington, D.C., as he said at the same speech:
☞ ". . . in regard to the abolition of slavery in the District of Columbia. . . . as a member of Congress, I should not with my present views be in favor of endeavoring to abolish slavery in the District of Columbia unless it would be upon these conditions: First, that the abolition should be gradual; second, that it should be on a vote of the majority of qualified voters in the District; and third, that compensation should be made to unwilling owners."[187]

☞ ". . . as to the question of the abolition of the slave-trade between the different States, I can truly answer, as I have, that I am pledged to nothing about it."[188]

☞ "When they [Southerners] remind us of their constitutional rights, I acknowledge them, not grudgingly, but fully, and fairly; and I would give them any legislation for the reclaiming of their [slave] fugitives . . ."[189]

Lincoln had held such views for most of his pre-presidential career. Far earlier, for example, in an October 3, 1845, letter to William Durley, Lincoln stated:
☞ "I hold it to be a paramount duty of us in the free States, due to the Union

of the States, and perhaps to liberty itself (paradox though it may seem), to let the slavery of the other States alone . . ."[190]

Lincoln believed, or more likely, pretended to believe, that the South wanted to "nationalize slavery"—an idea he called "the great Behemoth of danger"[191]—*and allow it to expand across the entire United States.*[192] *The truth is that the Confederacy, whose main focus was self-determination and states' rights, merely wanted the individual states—not the central government at Washington, D.C.—to decide for themselves whether to allow or prohibit slavery within their borders. Still, the Northern president kept up his anti-South lie that the Confederacy was pushing to make the U.S. a nation of slave states. What is revealing about the following statement from September 15, 1858, is that Lincoln does not ask for the destruction of slavery, only for the restriction of slavery to where it was already found, that is, in the South:*

☞ "All I have asked or desired anywhere is that it [slavery] should be placed back again upon the basis that the fathers of our government originally placed it upon. I have no doubt that it would become extinct, for all time to come, if we but readopted the policy of the fathers by restricting it to the limits it has already covered—restricting it from the new Territories."[193]

On September 16, 1858, Lincoln scrawled out the following note for possible use in future speeches:

☞ "I believe . . . that by our form of government the States which have slavery are to retain or disuse it, at their own pleasure; and that all others—individuals, free States, and National Government—are constitutionally bound to leave them alone about it. That our government was thus framed because of the necessity springing from the actual presence of slavery when it was formed."[194]

Two years later, on October 23, 1860, Lincoln, now the Republican (then Liberal) candidate for president, wrote a letter to William S. Speer that reads:

☞ "My dear Sir: Yours of the 13th was duly received. I appreciate your motive when you suggest the propriety of my writing for the public something disclaiming all intention to interfere with slaves or slavery in the States; but in my judgment it would do no good. I have already done this many, many times; and it is in print, and open to all who will read. Those who will not read or heed what I have already publicly said would not read or heed a repetition of it. . . . Yours truly, A. Lincoln."¹⁹⁵

During his fourth debate with Douglas on September 18, 1858, at Charleston, Illinois, Lincoln reiterated his stand that halting the spread of slavery, not outright abolition, was the best course of action for the United States:
☞ "I say, then, there is no way of putting an end to the slavery agitation amongst us but to put it back upon the basis where our fathers placed it, no way but to keep it out of our new Territories—to restrict it forever to the old States where it now exists."¹⁹⁶

On December 15, 1860, Lincoln replied to a letter from North Carolinian John A. Gilmer. In it he attempts to allay the South's fears that he would either interfere with or abolish slavery. He also makes an astonishing admission, saying that the only "substantial difference" between the North and the South is that the former wants to restrict slavery, the latter wants to extend it:
☞ "My dear Sir: Yours of the 10ᵗʰ is received. I am greatly disinclined to write a letter on the subject embraced in yours; and I would not do so, even privately as I do, were it not that I fear you might misconstrue my silence. . . . Do the people of the South really entertain fears that a Republican [then a Liberal] administration would, directly or indirectly, interfere with the slaves, or with them about the slaves? If they do, I wish to assure you, as once a friend, and still, I hope, not an enemy, that there is no cause for such fears. The South would be in no more danger in this respect than it was in the days of [George] Washington. I suppose, however, this does not meet the case. You think slavery is right and ought to be extended, while we think it is wrong and ought to be restricted. That, I suppose, is the rub. It certainly is the only substantial difference between us. Yours very truly, A. Lincoln."¹⁹⁷

To reemphasize, "Honest Abe," for once being completely honest, ends his letter to Gilmer with this sensational remark: To extend or restrict. This is the "only substantial difference between us." Thus, just prior to his War, Lincoln held that the only real conflict between the South's view of slavery and the North's was that the former wanted

to allow it to spread (mainly into the new Western Territories), while the latter wanted to contain it where it already existed (that is, in the South). No mention of emancipation or abolition. Just limitation. A few months later, on March 4, 1861, he would repeat the same sentiment almost word for word in his First Inaugural Address:
☞ "One section of our country believes slavery . . . ought to be extended, while the other believes it . . . ought not . . . be extended. This is the only substantial dispute."[198]

On September 16, 1859, in a speech at Columbus, Ohio, Lincoln voiced his concerns about the expansion of slavery and a "flood" of blacks "pouring" northward. If the institution is allowed to spread across the U.S., he said fearfully:
☞ "They will be ready for Jeff Davis and [Alexander H.] Stephens and other leaders of that company, to sound the bugle for the revival of the slave-trade, for the second Dred Scott decision, for the flood of slavery to be poured over the Free States [the North], while we shall be here tied down and helpless, and run over like sheep."[199]

On October 16, 1854, during a speech at Peoria, Illinois, the real reason for Lincoln's opposition to both slavery and to its expansion was finally revealed in all of its undisguised glory. Said the racist president:
☞ "Whether slavery shall go into Nebraska, or other new Territories, is not a matter of exclusive concern to the people who may go there. The whole nation is interested that the best use shall be made of the Territories. *We want them for homes of free white people.* This cannot be, to any considerable extent, if slavery shall be planted within them [emphasis added]."[200]

During the same address Lincoln wanted to be sure that his constituents understood that while he was for restricting the spread of slavery he was definitely not for racial equality:
☞ "Let it not be said I am contending for the establishment of political and social equality between the whites and blacks. I have already said the contrary. I am not now combating the argument of necessity, arising from the fact that the blacks are already among us; but I am combating what is set up as moral argument for allowing them to be taken where they have never

yet been—arguing against the extension of a bad thing, which where it already exists, we must of necessity, manage as we best can."²⁰¹

As a white supremacist and white separatist, Lincoln was very concerned over the increase in population of American blacks, as he notes in the same speech:
☞ "[One of the Conservatives' favorite but faulty arguments] is, that taking slaves to new countries does not increase their number. . . . There is some truth in this, and I am glad of it, but it is not wholly true. The African slave trade is not yet effectually suppressed [in the North]; and if we make a reasonable deduction for the white people amongst us, who are foreigners, and the descendants of foreigners, arriving here since 1808, *we shall find the increase of the black population out-running that of the white, to an extent unaccountable*, except by supposing that some of them too, have been coming from Africa. If this be so, the opening of new countries to the institution, increases the demand for, and augments the price of slaves, and so does, in fact, make slaves of freemen by causing them to be brought from Africa, and sold into bondage [emphasis added]."²⁰²

Lincoln's views concerning slavery were positively casual at times, as this October 13, 1858, remark at Quincy, Illinois, shows:
☞ "We [Liberals] . . . oppose it as an evil so far as it seeks to spread itself. We insist on the policy that shall restrict it to its present limits. We don't suppose that in doing this we violate anything due to the actual presence of the institution, or anything due to the constitutional guaranties thrown around it."²⁰³

---

*More than once Lincoln suggested that he might not issue any proclamation to free the slaves.*²⁰⁴ *Even after it was issued, originally, by his own orders, the Emancipation Proclamation was supposed to be temporary, not permanent: he said it would cease when the South (or individual states) surrendered.*²⁰⁵ *He then offered the Confederacy "liberal terms on . . . substantial and collateral points."*²⁰⁶ *What were these points?*
   At least one of them was allowing any Southern state returning to the Union to continue practicing slavery within its borders. Lincoln demanded only one thing: slaves who were already free could not be reenslaved, for eventually he wanted to be able to

deport them to Liberia.²⁰⁷ *As for those still under slavery, he said he would leave their fate to their individual state governments,*²⁰⁸ a states' right he had been defending for many years prior to the War.²⁰⁹ In essence, in the summer and fall of 1864, complete and full emancipation was not absolutely necessary to Lincoln if a Confederate state would simply surrender peacefully, rejoin the Union,²¹⁰ and pay its taxes.²¹¹

Seward confirmed this, stating that the effect of the Emancipation Proclamation and other "war measures" would end with the fighting. Thus it is patently clear then that Lincoln originally intended that the institution of slavery would be reestablished after the South's defeat, or if and when it capitulated.²¹²

Further evidence of this is supplied by Lincoln's "Ten Percent Plan," issued in December 1863.²¹³ Here a Confederate state could be "readmitted" to the Union if just 10 percent of its citizens took an oath of allegiance to the U.S. Afterward that state could reestablish slavery if it so desired (naturally, none were interested).²¹⁴ On June 9, 1864, Lincoln made reference to his failed Ten Percent Plan in his "Reply to the Committee Notifying President Lincoln of his Renomination":

☞ "I will say now . . . I approve the declaration in favor of so amending the Constitution as to prohibit slavery throughout the nation. When the people in revolt [that is, in the Confederacy], with a hundred days of explicit notice that *they could within those days resume their allegiance without the overthrow of their institution*, and that they could not so resume it afterward, elected to stand out [that is, reject it], such amendment of the Constitution as now proposed became a fitting and necessary conclusion to the final success of the Union cause [emphasis added]."²¹⁵

The president backed up such views with numerous other statements. On August 17, 1864, for instance, he responded to an attack charging him with demanding complete emancipation in all Southern states. This was incorrect, as he pointed out in a letter to Charles D. Robinson. Here, Lincoln states that he is wide open to any suggestions from Confederate President Jefferson Davis, including those regarding slavery:

☞ "My dear Sir: Your letter of the seventh was placed in my hand yesterday by [Wisconsin] Governor [Alexander] Randall. To me it seems plain that saying reunion and abandonment of slavery would be considered, if offered, is not saying that nothing else or less would be considered, if offered. But I will not stand upon the mere construction of language. It is true, as you remind me, that in the Greeley letter of 1862 I said: 'If I could save the Union without freeing any slave I would do it; and if I could save it by freeing all the slaves I would do it; and if I could save it by freeing some and leaving others alone I would also do that.' I continued in the same letter as follows: 'What I do about slavery and the colored race, I do because I believe it helps to save the Union; and what I forbear, I forbear because I do not believe it would help to save the Union. I shall do less whenever I shall believe what I am doing hurts the cause; and I shall do more whenever I shall believe doing more will help the cause.'

"All this I said in the utmost sincerity; and I am as true to the whole of it now as when I first said it. When I afterward proclaimed emancipation, and employed colored soldiers [in the army], I only followed the declaration just quoted from the Greeley letter that 'I shall do more whenever I shall believe doing more will help the cause.' The way these measures were to help the cause was not to be by magic or miracles, but by inducing the colored people to come bodily over from the rebel side to ours. . . . Drive back to the support of the rebellion the physical force which the colored people now give and promise us, and neither the present, nor any coming, administration can save the Union. Take from us and give to the enemy the hundred and thirty, forty, or fifty thousand colored persons now serving us as soldiers, seamen, and laborers, and we cannot longer maintain the contest. The party who could elect a President on a War and Slavery Restoration platform would, of necessity, lose the colored force; and that force being lost, would be as powerless to save the Union as to do any other impossible thing.

"It is not a question of sentiment or taste, but one of physical force, which may be measured and estimated, as horse-power and steampower are measured and estimated. And, by measurement, it is more than we can lose and live. Nor can we, by discarding it, get a white force in place of it. There is a witness in every white man's bosom that he would rather go to the war having the negro to help him than to help the enemy against him. It is not the giving of one class for another—it is simply giving a large force to the enemy for nothing in return. . . . If Jefferson Davis wishes for himself, or for the benefit of his friends at the North, to know what I would do if he were to offer peace and reunion, saying nothing about slavery, let him try me."[216]

On October 15, 1858, at Alton, Illinois, during his seventh and last debate with Douglas, Lincoln said:

☞ "Now, irrespective of the moral aspect of this question as to whether there is a right or wrong in enslaving a negro, *I am still in favor of our new Territories being in such a condition that white men may find a home*—may find some spot where they can better their condition—where they can settle upon new soil, and better their condition in life. I am in favor of this not merely (I must say it here as I have elsewhere) for our own people who are born amongst us, but *as an outlet for free white people everywhere*, the world over—in which Hans, and Baptiste, and Patrick, and all other men from all the world, may find new homes and better their condition in life [emphasis added]."[217]

It is here that we finally uncover the reason Lincoln himself was not involved in slavery, as so many other Yankees were—such as Ulysses S. Grant,[218] *Winfield Scott, David G. Farragut, George H. Thomas, and the family of Lincoln's wife, Mary Todd.*[219] *It is here that we come to the very foundation of his antislavery views and of his Emancipation Proclamation. It was not so much slavery itself that bothered him. It was that the institution brought whites and blacks into close proximity with one another, the latter "degrading" and "disgracing" the former, as Lincoln's associate David Wilmot once put it.*[220] *As Lincoln openly avows above, he wants the new Western Territories set aside for whites, "irrespective of the moral aspect of this question as to whether there is a right or wrong in enslaving a negro." Thus to keep America white (one of Lincoln's stated lifelong goals),*[221] *slavery would have to be limited (restriction) and abolished (emancipation), then blacks would have to be deported to a foreign land (colonization).*[222] *Restriction. Emancipation. Colonization. Here is Lincoln' true plan for slavery and the black man, all clearly mapped out for the entire world to see. On February 1, 1861, Lincoln wrote the following to his future secretary of state, William H. Seward:*

☞ "I say now . . . as I have all the while said, that on the territorial question—that is, the question of extending slavery under the national auspices—I am inflexible. I am for no compromise which assists or permits the extension of the institution on soil owned by the nation. And any trick by which the nation is to acquire territory, and then allow some local authority to spread slavery over it, is as obnoxious as any other. I take it that to effect some such result as this, and to put us again on the highroad to a slave empire, is the object of all these proposed compromises. I am against it. . . . Nor do I care much about New Mexico, if further extension were hedged against."[223]

Lincoln was so obsessed with restricting slavery to the South that he claimed that his party, the Republican (Liberal) Party, was formed for the sole purpose of preventing this very thing from happening. As he wrote in early December 1859 in a note for future speeches:

☞ "Purpose of the Republican organization.—The Republican party believe there is danger that slavery will be further extended, and ultimately made national in the United States; and to prevent this incidental and final consummation, is the purpose of this organization."[224]

Lincoln was a strong supporter of the Wilmot Proviso. Introduced in 1846 by Northern Liberal Representative David Wilmot, its purpose was to try and prevent the spread of slavery into Western lands acquired by the U.S. from Mexico during the Mexican-American War (1846-1848).[225] His proposition was not for the sake of blacks, however. It was solely for whites.[226] In 1847 Wilmot clarified his position, saying:

> "I plead the cause and the rights of white freemen. I would preserve to free white labor a fair country, a rich inheritance, where the sons of toil, of my own race and own color, can live without the disgrace which association with negro slavery brings upon free labor."[227]

Lincoln could not have agreed more with Wilmot, and in fact, according to his own statement on August 24, 1855, he voted for the anti-black, pro-white Wilmot Proviso on dozens of occasions:

☞ "When I was at Washington, I voted for the Wilmot proviso as good as forty times; . . . I now do no more than oppose the extension of slavery."[228]

In the same speech Lincoln went on to say:

☞ "Much as I hate slavery, I would consent to the extension of it rather than see the Union dissolved, just as I would consent to any great evil to avoid a greater one."[229]

On February 27, 1860, during his renowned Cooper Union Speech in New York, Lincoln states that slavery should continue to be protected under the Constitution. His only stipulation is that it should "not be extended" beyond where it was already permitted:

☞ "This is all Republicans [Liberals] ask—all Republicans desire—in relation to slavery. As those [Founding] fathers marked it, so let it be again marked, as an evil not to be extended, but to be tolerated and protected only because of and so far as its actual presence among us makes that toleration and protection a necessity. Let all the guaranties those fathers gave it be not grudgingly, but fully and fairly, maintained."[230]

Lincoln goes on to enthusiastically quote one of "those fathers," Thomas Jefferson, stressing his own personal beliefs pertaining to white supremacy, the emancipation and deportation of freed slaves, and the restriction of slavery to the South:[231]

☞ [Lincoln quoting Jefferson] "'It is still in our power to direct the process of emancipation and deportation peaceably, and in such slow degrees, as that the evil will wear off sensibly; and their places be . . . filled up by free white laborers. If, on the contrary, it is left to force itself on, human nature must shudder at the prospect held up.'"[232]

In the same speech Lincoln again asserts that he is not interested in abolition, but merely in restricting the spread of slavery:

☞ "Wrong as we think slavery is, we can yet afford to let it alone where it is, because that much is due to the necessity arising from its actual presence in the nation; but can we, while our votes will prevent it, allow it to spread into the national Territories, and to overrun us here in these free States?"[233]

On December 11, 1860, President-elect Lincoln wrote to William Kellogg:

☞ "Entertain no proposition for a compromise in regard to the extension of slavery. The instant you do they have us under again; all our labor is lost, and sooner or later must be done over. . . . Have none of it. The tug has to come, and better now than later."[234]

Contrary to the teachings of the anti-South movement, it is well known to slavery scholars that native Africans were never taken from Africa and sold to Yankee slave traders as free individuals. They were purchased from native slave traders, already enslaved by their African owners.[235] *Even Lincoln was aware of this, as he stated in his October 16, 1854, speech at Peoria, Illinois:*

☞ ". . . the African slave-trader . . . does not catch free negroes and bring them here. He finds them already slaves in the hands of their black captors, and he honestly buys them at the rate of about a red cotton handkerchief a head. This is very cheap, and it is a great abridgement of the sacred right of self-government to hang men for engaging in this profitable trade."²³⁶

On October 1, 1858, Lincoln scribbled out the following idea, for use in his senatorial debates against Stephen A. Douglas:
☞ "When, as in his last Springfield speech, he declares that I say, unless I shall play my batteries successfully, so as to abolish slavery in every one of the States, the Union shall be dissolved, he is absolutely bursting with conscience. It is nothing that I have never said any such thing."²³⁷

For those who still find it hard to accept that Lincoln was not an abolitionist, consider a meeting he attended on February 27, 1861. It was here, just two months before the start of the Civil War, that the president-elect met with a Southern peace delegation in Washington, D.C. that included Charles S. Morehead and William C. Rives. In their attempt to avert war with the U.S., the Confederate envoy pleaded with Lincoln to withdraw his troops from Fort Sumter and promise the Border States that they would be safe within the Union. Lincoln replied that he would not yield on blocking the expansion of slavery into the Western Territories (as this was always his ultimate goal regarding the institution). But, he added, he would most certainly be willing to approve a constitutional amendment allowing slavery to continue indefinitely where it already existed. And he wasted no time in standing behind his promise.²³⁸

Lincoln's proposed amendment, the Corwin Amendment (named after Ohio Liberal Thomas Corwin, who introduced it to Congress), allowed slavery to continue in perpetuity without any interference from the U.S. government. It was passed by the U.S. House of Representatives the very next day (February 28, 1861), and by the U.S. Senate on March 2, 1861, two days before his presidential inauguration.²³⁹ By this time three states had actually ratified the amendment, and certainly the rest would have as well, if given the chance. However, the act was dropped with the start of the Battle of Fort Sumter, on April 12, 1861. Had hostilities not exploded between the South and the North that Spring day, what can only be called Lincoln's "proslavery amendment" would have been signed into law, and American slavery would have continued indefinitely.²⁴⁰

Thus, while Lincoln sometimes preached against slavery in public in the North, behind closed doors he was trying to use the Constitution to make the institution "irrevocable"—permitting slavery, in fact, to persist as long as the Southern states returned to the Union, remained,[241] and paid their taxes.[242]

Two days later, in his First Inaugural Address, March 4, 1861, Lincoln reiterated his views on the subject. As he often did, he opens with an outrageous lie, in this case pretending to know nothing about his own amendment. However, he ends by emphatically stating that he supports it. In plain English, Lincoln says here that he supports the idea of an amendment that would forever prohibit the U.S. government from interfering with slavery:

☞ "I understand *a proposed amendment to the Constitution*—which amendment, however, I have not seen—has passed Congress, to the effect that *the Federal Government shall never interfere with the domestic institutions* [that is, slavery] *of the States, including that of persons held to service* [that is, slaves]. To avoid misconstruction of what I have said, I depart from my purpose not to speak of particular amendments so far as to say that, holding such a provision to now be implied constitutional law, *I have no objection to its being made express and irrevocable* [emphasis added]."[243]

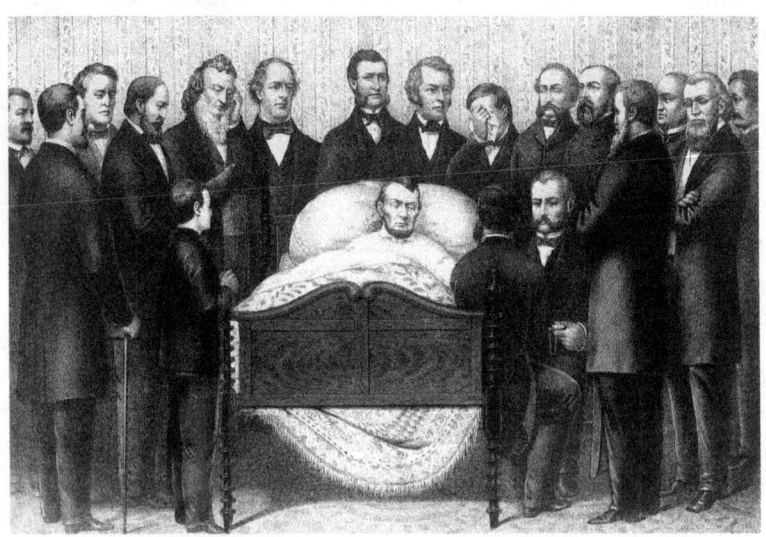

It was not Lincoln's fake and illegal Final Emancipation Proclamation, issued on January 1, 1863, that finally freed African-Americans from the shackles of both slavery and a largely racist white Northern society. It was the president's death, depicted here, on April 15, 1865. For, as his own words reveal, it was Lincoln who consistently blocked the advancement of blacks, refused to grant them the vote, denied them citizenship, and would not see them as equals. If there was a "Great Emancipator," it was certainly not Lincoln. If anything it was the bullet fired from the gun of John Wilkes Booth, for full and complete black civil rights came only *after* Lincoln died.

THE GETTYSBURG ADDRESS

TODAY THE GETTYSBURG ADDRESS IS considered by many to be Lincoln's finest speech. Delivered at the dedication of the cemetery at Gettysburg, Pennsylvania, on November 19, 1863, entire books have been written about it. As such it is commonly assumed that it was received with rapt attention, constant cheers, tear swollen eyes, and thunderous applause. The truth, from Lincoln himself, is quite different, however.

Here is what the president told his friends afterward:
☞ ". . . that speech fell on the audience like a wet blanket. I am distressed about it. . . ."[244] "It is a flat failure and the people are disappointed."[245]

We should not be surprised that it "fell on the audience like a wet blanket." As even Lincoln's Northern audience at the time well understood, the Gettysburg Address is one of the most faithless, cynical, erroneous, and cruelly ironic speeches ever uttered, for in it the Constitution-loathing Liberal promises to uphold the Constitution, when in fact he did the opposite.[246] He blames the South for the War, when it was a conflict that he not only wanted but that he also nefariously instigated.[247] He also praises America's true political heritage. Yet two years later, on April 9, 1865, at Appomattox,[248] he overturned it, then caused it to "perish from the earth." What was that political heritage? It was not a "new nation," as Lincoln calls it. It was our original Jeffersonian Confederate Republic—a voluntary Union of friendly states based on states' rights; a constitutional government "of the people, by the people, for the people."[249]

Here is what Maryland journalist H. L. Mencken had to say about Lincoln's most famous declamation:

> The Gettysburg speech was at once the shortest and the most famous oration in American history. . . . the highest emotion reduced to a few poetical phrases. Lincoln himself never even remotely approached it. It is genuinely stupendous. But let us not forget that it is poetry, not logic; beauty, not sense. Think of the argument in it. Put it into the cold words of everyday. The doctrine is simply this: that the Union soldiers who died at Gettysburg sacrificed their lives to the cause of self-determination—that government of the people, by the people, for the people, should not perish from the earth. It is difficult to imagine anything more untrue. The Union soldiers [Liberals] in the battle actually fought against self-determination; it was the Confederates [Conservatives] who fought for the right of their people to govern themselves.[250]

During his Second Inaugural Address on March 4, 1865 (shown here), Lincoln once again lied to the American public, not only claiming that the South started the War, but that she was trying to "strengthen, perpetuate, and extend" slavery. Both statements are historically and demonstrably false. The president is in the center, standing behind the small white podium.

Noted British journalist Alistair Cooke agrees, calling Lincoln's Gettysburg Address a classic work of oratory of highly questionable reasoning.[251] How true. Naturally, the Victorian Americans who listened to the speech that Autumn day in Pennsylvania had not yet been blinded by the anti-South movement's postwar political deification of Lincoln. Instead, they saw him simply as what he was: a demagogic rhetorician reciting vacuous nonsense in an attempt to maintain support for his illicit War on the South and states' rights. Thus, Lincoln should not have expected his little speech to be anything but a "flat failure" and a "disappointment to the people."

10

THE SOUTHERN PEOPLE

DID LINCOLN HATE THE SOUTH? Those of us who live in the South, where we are still recovering from the terrible widespread damage caused by Lincoln's War, would answer with a resounding "yes!"[252] However, in his speeches Lincoln at times evinced a tender sympathy with Dixie, which one might expect considering he was born in Kentucky.

In an August 21, 1858, speech at Ottawa, Illinois, Lincoln was uncharacteristically empathetic toward his Southern brothers and sisters:

☞ "Before proceeding, let me say I think I have no prejudice against the Southern people. They are just what we would be in their situation. If slavery did not now exist amongst them, they would not introduce it. If it did now exist amongst us, we should not instantly give it up. This I believe of the masses north and south. Doubtless there are individuals, on both sides, who would not hold slaves under any circumstances; and others who would gladly introduce slavery anew, if it were out of existence. We know that some southern men do free their slaves, go north, and become tip-top abolitionists; while some northern ones go south, and become most cruel slave-masters.

"When southern people tell us they are no more responsible for the origin of slavery than we, I acknowledge the fact. When it is said that the institution exists, and that it is very difficult to get rid of it, in any satisfactory way, I can understand and appreciate the saying. I surely will not blame them for not doing what I should not know how to do myself."[253]

From an October 16, 1854, speech:

☞ "[Concerning Southern slave owners, it] is kindly provided that of all those who come into the world, only a small percentage are natural tyrants. That percentage is no larger in the slave States than in the free. The great majority, south as well as north, have human sympathies, of which they can no more divest themselves than they can of their sensibility to physical pain. These sympathies in the bosoms of the southern people, manifest in many ways, their sense of the wrong of slavery, and their consciousness that, after all, there is humanity in the negro."[254]

Despite these seemingly tender sentiments, three years later Lincoln used what he ludicrously called his "better angel"[255] to viciously and illegitimately invade the South, using a scorched earth policy of total war to destroy her infrastructure, and burn her homes, shops, towns, schools, churches, hospitals, libraries, and universities to the ground, killing nearly two million (one million Southern whites and one million Southern blacks) of her people in the process. Horribly, most of these were non-combatants, as almost all civilian deaths during the War occurred in the South.[256]

Why did Lincoln say one thing and do another? Why did he claim to have "no prejudice against the Southern people," then turn around and bomb them into submission? Our warmongering sixteenth president took the answer to his grave.

Lincoln's home, Springfield, Illinois. The original 19th-Century caption reads: "He left it in peace to preside over a nation, then in bondage. He now reposes under its soil a martyr to the Freedom he won." Lincoln's own words establish that neither of these statements are true.

AFRICAN AMERICANS AND WHITE RACISM

FOR THE PAST 150 YEARS Abraham Lincoln has been repeatedly cast as the "Great Emancipator" and the "true friend of the black man." Was he? Not according to the following quotes made by the president, none of which they want you to find out about. Why? Because knowing how Liberal Lincoln really felt about African-Americans would expose the truth behind his unconstitutional War on the conservative South.

In a conversation that Yankee lawyer Edward L. Pierce once had with Lincoln, he reported that the president unashamedly referred to blacks as "niggers" rather than as Negroes.[257] We should not be shocked at Lincoln's use of such language. After all, this is the same man who referred to Mexicans as "greasers,"[258] "mongrels,"[259] and also inevitably as an "inferior race," as he called all non-white peoples.[260] What is shocking is that Lincoln continues to be lovingly referred to as a "humanitarian," an "egalitarian," the "true friend of the black man," and the "Great Emancipator."

One of the earliest public statements Lincoln made concerning his beliefs about white supremacy came on June 13, 1836, when he made an announcement declaring his political views in the local paper, the Illinois Sangamon Journal. Though blacks, enslaved and free, certainly "bore the burden" of helping settle, develop, and maintain the United States through their many contributions, Lincoln did not feel they deserved to "share the privileges" of its government:

☞ "To the Editor of the *Journal*: In your paper of last Saturday I see a communication, over the signature of 'Many Voters,' in which the candidates who are announced in the *Journal* are called upon to 'show their hands.' Agreed. Here's mine.

"I go for all sharing the privileges of the government who assist in bearing its burdens. Consequently, I go for admitting all whites to the right of suffrage who pay taxes or bear arms . . ."[261]

In September 1859, just a year before he was elected president, atheist Lincoln was asked how he felt about the idea of equal rights for blacks, to which he replied:
☞ "Negro equality! Fudge!! How long, in the Government of a God great enough to make and maintain this universe, shall there continue [to be] knaves to vend and fools to gulp, so low a piece of demagoguism as this?"[262]

On August 21, 1858, during one of his public debates with Stephen A. Douglas at Ottawa, Illinois, Lincoln not only agreed with his opponent's call for continued white supremacy, he also complained that he had been misrepresented as having promoted interracial marriage. In response, he angrily denied the charge, saying that he had never intended to
☞ "set the niggers and white people to marry together."[263]

At the same debate Lincoln declared:
☞ ". . . this is the true complexion of all I have ever said in regard to the institution of slavery and the black race. This is the whole of it, and anything that argues me into this idea of perfect, social, and political equality with the negro, is but a specious and fantastic arrangement of words, by which a man can prove a horse chestnut to be a chestnut horse."[264]

Again, during his August 21, 1858, debate, Lincoln touched on the topic of nationalizing slavery. As we have seen, he was not against slavery. As a white separatist he was merely against it spreading outside the South and into the "lily-white North." To assuage the fears of his supporters in the audience, he assured them that not even war could extend slavery beyond the borders of the Southern states. As he put it:
☞ "In the first place, what is necessary to make the institution national? Not war. There is no danger that the people of Kentucky will shoulder their muskets, and, with a young nigger stuck on every bayonet, march into Illinois

and force them upon us. There is no danger of our going over there and making war upon them."²⁶⁵

Lincoln here went on to answer Douglas' charge, that he was trying to establish racial equality, with this remark:
☞ "I had no thought in the world that I was doing anything to bring about a political and social equality of the black and white races."²⁶⁶

A month earlier, on July 10, 1858, at Chicago, Illinois, Lincoln gave a speech in which he replied to further accusations made by Douglas, among them that he was a "negro-worshiper."²⁶⁷ Infuriated, the white separatist and supporter of American apartheid responded this way:
☞ "We were often—more than once at least—in the course of Judge Douglas's speech last night reminded that this government was made for white men—that he believed it was made for white men. Well, that is putting it into a shape in which no one wants to deny it; but the judge then goes into his passion for drawing inferences that are not warranted. I protest, now and forever, against that counterfeit logic which presumes that because I do not want a negro woman for a slave, I do necessarily want her for a wife. My understanding is that I need not have her for either; but, as God made us separate, we can leave one another alone, and do one another much good thereby. There are white men enough to marry all the white women, and enough black men to marry all the black women, and in God's name let them be so married. The judge regales us with the terrible enormities that take place by the mixture of races: that the inferior race bears the superior down. Why, judge, if we do not let them get together in the Territories, they won't mix there. [An audience member: "Three cheers for Lincoln!" The cheers were given with a hearty good will.] I should say at least that that is a self-evident truth."²⁶⁸

Is this attitude surprising? By now it should not be. This is the same man who, on October 16, 1854, said the following:
☞ "In the course of his reply, Senator Douglas remarked, in substance, that he had always considered this government was made for the white people and

not for the negroes. Why, in point of mere fact, I think so too."²⁶⁹

Lincoln was never hesitant to use the "n" word, even after he became president. Sometime, in the summer of 1861, Liberal U.S. Congressman James Mitchell Ashley recorded the following conversation with the Yankee chief executive, in which they discussed so-called "Reconstruction":

☞ [Ashley speaking] "After an unusually long and warm discussion one morning on this subject, I rose to go, quite dissatisfied with the result of my interview and exhibiting a little more feeling than I ought, when the President called out, and said: 'Ashley, that was a great speech you made out in Ohio the other day.' I turned, and, I fear with some irritation in both manner and voice, said: 'I have made no speech anywhere, Mr. President, and have not been out of Washington.' He laughed and said: 'Well, I see Nasby says that in consequence of one speech made by Jim Ashley, four hundred thousand niggers moved into Wood County last week, and it must have taken a great speech to do that.' Of course I joined in the laugh, and then Mr. Lincoln, in his kindly manner, said: 'Come up soon, Ashley, and we will take up reconstruction again.'"²⁷⁰

The following fragment of one of Lincoln's speeches, from September 8, 1858, at Paris, Illinois, reveals that the soon-to-be president was actually very comfortable using the word "nigger", whether coming from his own lips, or quoting someone else:

☞ "Was it the right of emigrants to Kansas and Nebraska to govern themselves, and a lot of 'niggers,' too, if they wanted them? Clearly this was no invention of his [Stephen A. Douglas], because General [Lewis] Cass put forth the same doctrine in 1848 in his so-called Nicholson letter, six years before Douglas thought of such a thing. Then what was it that the 'Little Giant' invented? It never occurred to General Cass to call his discovery by the odd name of popular sovereignty. He had not the face to say that the right of the people to govern 'niggers' was the right of the people to govern themselves. His notions of the fitness of things were not moulded to the brazenness of calling the right to put a hundred 'niggers' through under the lash in Nebraska a 'sacred' right of self-government."²⁷¹

At Charleston, Illinois, during his fourth debate with Douglas, the "Little Giant," on September 18, 1858, Lincoln made the following remarks:

☞ "While I was at the hotel to-day, an elderly gentleman called upon me to know whether I was really in favor of producing a perfect equality between the negroes and white people. While I had not proposed to myself on this occasion to say much on that subject, yet as the question was asked me I thought I would occupy perhaps five minutes in saying something in regard to it. I will say then that I am not, nor ever have been, in favor of bringing about in any way the social and political equality of the white and black races—that I am not, nor ever have been, in favor of making voters or jurors of negroes, nor of qualifying them to hold office, nor to intermarry with white people. . ."[272]

☞ ". . . and I will say in addition to this that there is a physical difference between the white and black races which I believe will forever forbid the two races living together on terms of social and political equality. And inasmuch as they cannot so live, while they do remain together there must be the position of superior and inferior, and I as much as any other man am in favor of having the superior position assigned to the white race."[273]

☞ "I say upon this occasion I do not perceive that because the white man is to have the superior position the negro should be denied everything. I do not understand that because I do not want a negro woman for a slave I must necessarily want her for a wife. My understanding is that I can just let her alone. I am now in my fiftieth year, and I certainly never have had a black woman for either a slave or a wife. So it seems to me quite possible for us to get along without making either slaves or wives of negroes."[274]

☞ "I will add to this that I have never seen, to my knowledge, a man, woman, or child who was in favor of producing a perfect equality, social and political, between negroes and white men. I recollect of but one distinguished instance that I ever heard of so frequently as to be entirely satisfied of its correctness, and that is the case of Judge Douglas's old friend Colonel Richard M. Johnson."[275]

☞ "I will also add to the remarks I have made (for I am not going to enter at large upon this subject), that I have never had the least apprehension that I or my friends would marry negroes if there was no law to keep them from it; but as Judge Douglas and his friends seem to be in great apprehension that they might, if there were no law to keep them from it, I give him the most solemn pledge that I will to the very last stand by the law of this State, which forbids the marrying of white people with negroes."[276]

On October 18, 1858, from Springfield, Illinois, Lincoln wrote a letter to one J. N. Brown. Impatient with those who continually questioned and misunderstood him, the exasperated president again expanded on his racial feelings:
☞ "I do not perceive how I can express myself, more plainly, than I have done . . . I have expressly disclaimed all intention to bring about social and political equality between the white and black races . . . I say . . . that Congress, which lays the foundations of society, should . . . be strongly opposed to the incorporation of slavery among its elements. But it does not follow that social and political equality between whites and blacks, must be incorporated . . ."[277]

During the Lincoln-Douglas debates, tired of the constant accusations of being a "negro-worshiper,"[278] *Lincoln made this emphatic public reply in a September 16, 1859, speech at Columbus, Ohio:*
☞ "If there was a necessary conflict between the white man and the negro, I should be for the white man . . ."[279]

On February 27, 1860, Lincoln used a similar expression in his celebrated Cooper Union Speech in New York:
☞ "The proposition that there is a struggle between the white man and the negro contains a falsehood. There is no struggle. If there was, I should be for

the white man."²⁸⁰

Speaking as a Yankee to a group of Southerners on September 17, 1859, Lincoln declared:

☞ "We mean to marry your girls when we have a chance—the white ones, I mean . . ."²⁸¹

On September 15, 1858, at one of the Lincoln-Douglas Debates, Lincoln read a quote by newspaper editor Z. B. Mayo of DeKalb County, Illinois, adding his own comment at the end (in italics):

☞ [Quoting Mayo] "'Our opinion is that it would be best for all concerned to have the colored population in a State by themselves' [*in this I agree with him* (Lincoln's note)]."²⁸²

Lincoln, like the black racists, black separatists, and black colonizationists who came before and after him,²⁸³ felt a deep repugnance toward those of other races.²⁸⁴ Thus, he believed that he had good reason for wanting to prevent blacks from voting, sitting on juries, holding political office, or marrying whites.²⁸⁵ Since, according to him, whites are the superior race and blacks the inferior, the mixing of the two could only lead to that most dreaded of all the racist's fears, what Victorian whites called "amalgamation"; that is, the interbreeding and intermarriage of the two races. Said Lincoln on June 26, 1857, in his famous Dred Scott Speech at Springfield, Illinois:

☞ "There is a natural disgust in the minds of nearly all white people, to the idea of an indiscriminate amalgamation of the white and black races; . . . Now I protest against that counterfeit logic which concludes that, because I do not want a black woman for a slave I must necessarily want her for a wife. I need not have her for either, I can just leave alone. In some respects she certainly is not my equal; but in her natural right the bread she earns with her own hands without asking leave of any one else, she is my equal, and the equal of all others."²⁸⁶

Based on Lincoln's own words and actions, it is obvious that he included himself in the category of *"nearly all white people."*[287] *(Let us note here that most Southern whites did not feel this way.)*[288] *Being from ultra Negrophobic Illinois—a state that even Lincoln admitted had more stringent anti-black laws than Louisiana*[289]*—the Yankee president had strong feelings about blocking the spread of slavery, not only from his state, but also from the Western Territories, for Illinois itself was considered a Western state at the time.*[290] On October 16, 1854, during a speech at Peoria, Illinois, for example, Lincoln could not have been more explicit:

☞ "Let it not be said I am contending for the establishment of political and social equality between the whites and blacks. I have already said the contrary. . . I am . . . arguing against the extension of a bad thing, which where it already exists, we must of necessity, manage as best we can."[291]

This is precisely why Liberal Lincoln had been against the Mexican-American War:[292] *unable to see it for what it actually was (a land war to expand U.S. territory; that is, an aspect of Manifest Destiny),*[293] *he mistakenly and irresponsibly viewed it as an intentional ploy by Conservatives, in particular Southern Conservatives, to spread slavery westward.*[294] *As he said on July 1, 1848:*

☞ "As to the Mexican war, I still think the defensive line policy the best to terminate it. In a final treaty of peace, we shall probably be under a sort of necessity of taking some territory; but it is my desire that we shall not acquire any extending so far south as to enlarge and aggravate the distracting question of slavery."[295]

During his June 26, 1857, Dred Scott Speech, Lincoln gives perhaps the primary reason he was against slavery to begin with: it brought the two races into close contact, potentially causing the "mixing of blood" through intimate contact. This helps explain Lincoln's bigoted obsession with eliminating the creation of more "mulattos":

☞ ". . . Judge Douglas is especially horrified at the thought of the mixing of blood by the white and black races. Agreed for once—a thousand times agreed. There are white men enough to marry all the white women, and black men enough to marry all the black women; and so let them be married. On this point we fully agree with the judge, and when he shall show that his policy is better adapted to prevent amalgamation than ours, we shall drop ours and adopt his. Let us see. In 1850 there were in the United States 405,751 *mulattos*. Very few of these are the offspring of whites and free blacks; nearly all have sprung from black slaves and white masters. *A separation of the races is the only perfect preventive of* amalgamation; but as an immediate separation is impossible, the next best thing is to keep them apart where they are not already together. *If white and black people never get together in Kansas, they will never mix blood in Kansas.* That is at least one self-evident truth. A few free colored persons may get into the free States, in any event; but their number is too insignificant to amount to much in the way of *mixing blood*. In 1850 there were in the free States 56,649 *mulattos*; but for the most part they were not born there—they came from the slave States, ready made up. In the same year the slave States had 348,874 *mulattos*, all of home production. *The proportion of free mulattos to free blacks*—the only colored classes in the free States—is much greater in the slave than in the free States. It is worthy of note, too, that among the free States those which make the colored man the nearest equal to the white have proportionably the fewest *mulattos*, the least of amalgamation. In New Hampshire, the State which goes farthest toward equality between the races, there are just 184 *mulattos*, while there are in Virginia—how many do you think?—79,775, being 23,126 more than in all the free States together.

"These statistics show that *slavery is the greatest source of amalgamation*, and next to it, not the elevation, but the degradation of the free blacks. Yet Judge Douglas dreads the slightest restraints on the spread of slavery, and the slightest human recognition of the negro, as tending horribly to *amalgamation*.

"The very Dred Scott case affords a strong test as to which party most favors amalgamation, the Republicans [Liberals] or the dear Union-saving Democracy [Conservatives]. Dred Scott, his wife, and two daughters were all involved in the suit. We desired the court to have held that they were citizens so far at least as to entitle them to a hearing as to whether they were free or not; and then, also, that they were in fact and in law really free. *Could we have had our way, the chances of these black girls ever mixing their blood with that of white people would have been diminished at least to the extent that it could not have been without their consent.* But Judge Douglas is delighted to have them decided to be slaves, and not human enough to have a hearing, even if they were free, and thus left subject to the forced concubinage of their masters, and liable to become the mothers of *mulattos* in spite of themselves: the very state of case that produces nine tenths of all the mulattos—all *the mixing of blood* in the nation.

"Of course, I state this case as an illustration only, not meaning to say or intimate that the master of Dred Scott and his family, or any more than a percentage of masters generally, are inclined to exercise this particular power which they hold over their female slaves.

"*I have said that the separation of the races is the only perfect preventive of amalgamation.* I have no right to say all the members of the Republican party are in favor of this, nor to say that as a party they are in favor or it. There is nothing in their platform directly on the subject. But I can say a very large proportion of its members are for it, and that the chief plank in their platform—opposition to the spread of slavery—is most favorable to that separation [emphasis added]."[296]

Lincoln goes on to discuss the deportation (known then as "colonization") of all freed blacks, his ideal solution to the "race problem":

☞ "Such separation, if ever effected at all, must be effected by colonization; and no political party, as such, is now doing anything directly for colonization. Party operations at present only favor or retard colonization incidentally. The enterprise is a difficult one; but 'where there is a will there is a way,' and what colonization needs most is a hearty will. Will springs from the two elements of moral sense and self-interest. Let us be brought to believe *it is morally right, and at the same time favorable to, or at least not against, our interest to transfer the African to his native clime, and we shall find a way to do it, however great the task may be.* The children of Israel, to such numbers as to include four hundred thousand fighting men, went out of Egyptian bondage in a body.

"How differently the respective courses of the Democratic and Republican parties incidentally bear on the question of forming a will—a public sentiment—for colonization, is easy to see [emphasis added]."[297]

At national conventions Lincoln's Liberal party leaders continually discussed their opposition to slavery and its extension. Not because they wanted to liberate the slaves or grant political or social equality to free blacks in the North,[298] *but because they wanted, in Lincoln's own words, to maintain "the superior position assigned to the white race."*[299] *Just because the Declaration of Independence states that "all men are created equal," he wrote to James N. Brown on October 18, 1858,*

☞ "it does not follow that social and political equality between white and black, must be incorporated, because slavery must not. The declaration does not require so."[300]

It is patently clear that as a white supremacist, Liberal Lincoln did not like non-white people, whom he routinely referred to as "inferior races."[301] Here, for instance, is what he had to say about Mexicans on October 7, 1858, during a public address at Galesburg, Illinois:

☞ "I understand that the people of Mexico are most decidedly a race of mongrels. I understand that there is not more than one person there out of eight who is a pure white . . ."[302]

Lincoln's *Final* Emancipation Proclamation, the infamous illegal document that freed no slaves and which he issued, in his own words, solely as a "military necessity" and a "war measure." The president's cabinet forced him to leave his colonization clause (in which he asked Congress to set aside funds for the deportation of American blacks) out of this particular version.

BLACK EQUAL RIGHTS

PRO-NORTH HISTORIANS TELL US THAT Lincoln was for giving equal rights to African-Americans in the Old North. Such rights would have included giving blacks the right to hold political office, sue in court, sit on juries, marry whites, sit next to whites in carriages, attend white schools and churches, vote (suffrage), and above all become American citizens (we will note here that in the far less racist, far more tolerant Old South, blacks already possessed many of these rights). [303]

Like most Northern Liberals at the time, Liberal Lincoln too was against all of these things, as the following forbidden quotes reveal.

───♦───

The truth that you will never read in books by Lincoln apologists, Lincoln worshipers, or pro-North/anti-South proponents is that it was Lincoln who was the main barrier against the abolition of slavery, against the granting of full civil rights to blacks, and against the incorporation of blacks into mainstream white America. All, in fact, came only after Lincoln died on April 15, 1865, inadvertently and ironically making John Wilkes Booth the true "Great Emancipator."[304]

Throughout his political career, for instance, Lincoln was repeatedly challenged as to whether he was in favor of "negro citizenship," and he repeatedly gave the same answer, as he did at Charleston, Illinois, on September 18, 1858, in a rebuttal to Stephen A. Douglas:

☞ "Judge Douglas has said to you that he has not been able to get from me an answer to the question whether I am in favor of negro citizenship. So far as I know, the judge never asked me the question before. He shall have no occasion to ever ask it again, for I tell him very frankly that *I am not in favor of negro citizenship.* This furnishes me an occasion for saying a few words upon the subject. I mentioned in a certain speech of mine, which has been printed, that the Supreme Court had decided that a negro could not possibly be made a citizen, and without saying what was my ground of complaint in regard to that, or whether I had any ground of complaint, Judge Douglas has from that thing manufactured nearly everything that he ever says about my disposition to produce an equality between the negroes and the white people. If any one will read my speech, he will find I mentioned that as one of the points decided in the course of the Supreme Court opinions, but I did not state what objection I had to it. But Judge Douglas tells the people what my objection was when I did not tell them myself. *Now my opinion is that the different States have the power to make a negro a citizen under the Constitution of the United States, if they choose. The Dred Scott decision decides that they have not that power. If the State of Illinois had that power, I should be opposed to the exercise of it. That is all I have to say about it* [emphasis added]."[305]

On July 17, 1858, at Springfield, Illinois, white supremacist Lincoln made this public announcement:

☞ "My declarations upon this subject of negro slavery may be misrepresented, but cannot be misunderstood. I have said that I do not understand the Declaration [of Independence] to mean that all men were created equal in all respects. . . . *Certainly the negro is not our equal in color—perhaps not in many other respects* . . . [emphasis added]"[306]

On September 16, 1859, at Columbus, Ohio, Lincoln once again publicly repeated a statement from an earlier address to reemphasize his position on race. Bear in mind that he would be nominated for president of the United States just eight months later, and that he would be elected president within 14 months of these comments:

☞ "I will say then that *I am not, nor ever have been, in favor of bringing about in any way the social and political equality of the white and black races*—that *I am not, nor ever have been, in favor of making voters or jurors of negroes, nor of qualifying them to hold office, nor to intermarry with white people*; and I will say in addition to this that *there is a physical difference between the white and black races, which, I believe, will forever forbid the two races living together on terms of social and political equality*. And *inasmuch as they cannot so live, while they do remain together there must be the position of superior and inferior, and I as much as any other man am in favor of having the superior position assigned to the white race* [emphasis added]."[307]

As we will recall from Chapter 7, in his October 16, 1854, speech at Peoria, Illinois, Lincoln brought up one of his favorite topics: black colonization, the deportation of all African-Americans to foreign colonies. After admitting that this would be a near impossible task, he then asks his audience rhetorically:

☞ "What then? Free them all, and keep them among us as underlings? Is it quite certain that this betters their condition? *I think I would not hold one in slavery, at any rate; yet the point is not clear enough for me to denounce people upon. What next? Free them, and make them politically and socially, our equals? My own feelings will not admit of this; and if mine would, we well know that those of the great mass of white people will not.* Whether this feeling accords with justice and sound judgment, is not the sole question, if indeed, it is any part of it. A universal feeling, whether well or ill-founded, can not be safely disregarded. *We can not, then, make them equals.* It does seem to me that systems of gradual emancipation might be adopted; but for their tardiness in this, I will not undertake to judge our brethren of the south [emphasis added]."[308]

On October 7, 1858, only two years before him became president, Lincoln made the following comment to his audience at Galesburg, Illinois:

☞ "I have all the while maintained that in so far as it should be insisted that there was an equality between the white and black races that should produce a perfect social and political equality, it was an impossibility."[309]

On September 8, 1858, during a speech at Clinton, Illinois, Lincoln responded to accusations that he and his party favored racial equality, a serious taboo in the North at the time:[310]

☞ "And now let me say a few words in regard to [Stephen A.] Douglas's great hobby of negro equality. He thinks—he says at least—that the Republican [Liberal] party is in favor of allowing whites and blacks to intermarry, and that a man can't be a good Republican unless he is willing to elevate black men to office and to associate with them on terms of perfect equality. He knows that we advocate no such doctrines as those . . ."[311]

At least in this one area Lincoln was consistent. *During his September 16, 1859, speech at Columbus, Ohio, he once again publicly denounced the idea of black suffrage:*

☞ "I did not at any time say I was in favor of negro suffrage; but the absolute proof that twice—once substantially and once expressly—I declared against it."³¹²

Not once did Lincoln ever publicly support the idea of giving all *American blacks the right to vote. For instance, on April 11, 1865, three days before his death from the assassin's bullet, Lincoln was still standing in the way of granting blacks the franchise.*

Today Lincoln is held up as the champion of African-Americans and black civil rights. His surviving writings, however, tell us that until the day he died he was a white supremacist who preferred living in an all-white America.

It was on this day that the president gave his last public speech. In it he deflected Yankee criticism that he still had not granted blacks total civil rights, obfuscating and wavering, finally deferring the entire issue to future generations. In his typically foggy and understated manner, Lincoln laconically told the crowd that he knew that it is unsatisfactory to some

☞ "that the elective franchise is not [yet] given to the colored man. I would myself prefer that it were now conferred on the very intelligent [blacks], and on those [blacks] who serve our cause as soldiers."³¹³

*Bizarrely, pro-Lincoln historians and scholars consider this the first time a U.S. president "endorsed black suffrage."*³¹⁴ *But was "preferring" to "confer" it only on the "very intelligent" and those who served as soldiers, while still refusing to give all other blacks the vote, really an endorsement? Hardly. Black Union soldiers comprised only a tiny minority of the total population of American blacks at the time.*³¹⁵ *And who was to decide which African-Americans were "very intelligent" and which were not? This was just more typical Lincolnian politics—concealed bigotry, muddling, trickery, delay tactics, and word twisting—from the North's most masterful spin doctor.*

13

BLACK COLONIZATION AND WHITE SEPARATISM

WHEN IT CAME TO AMERICAN blacks and slavery, Lincoln's views could not have been summed up any better than they were by his political idol, Kentucky slave owner Henry Clay, the Liberal instigator of the anti-American "American System," who once said:

"I desire no concealment of my opinions in regard to the institution of slavery. I look upon it as a great evil, and deeply lament that we have derived it from the parent government, and from our ancestors. *I wish every slave in the United States was in the country of his ancestors* [that is, Africa]. But here they are, and the question is, how can they be best dealt with? If a state of nature existed, and we were about to lay the foundations of society, no man would be more strongly opposed than I should be, to incorporating the institution of slavery among its elements [emphasis added]."[316]

To fully understand Clay's and Lincoln's absurd racist plans to deport American blacks and resettle them in colonies in Africa, Europe, the Caribbean, and South America, one need only examine the history of the American Colonization Society (ACS), of which Lincoln was an evangelistic and longstanding member.

The ACS was founded in 1816 in Washington, D.C., by a Northerner, New Jerseyan Reverend Robert Finley.[317] Among its early leaders, officers, and supporters were such famed Yankees as New England statesman Daniel Webster (after whom the town of Webster, Massachusetts, was named), New Yorker William H. Seward (Lincoln's secretary of state, and the man after whom the city of Seward, Alaska, and the Seward Peninsula were named), and Marylander Francis Scott Key (author of the U.S. National Anthem, *The Star-Spangled Banner*).³¹⁸

The nation's largest and most enthusiastic ACS chapter was in Boston, Massachusetts, where antislavery and anti-black sentiment were at their highest in the nation. The two were not mutually exclusive in New England,³¹⁹ for the Bay State was the birthplace of both the American slave trade (in 1638)³²⁰ and American slavery (in 1641).³²¹

The stated mission of the ACS was the preservation of white culture through the deportation of all American blacks, both free and emancipated, out of the U.S. The African colony of Liberia was created by the ACS in 1822 for this very purpose: to "liberate" America from blacks, hence its name.³²²

One of the most passionate members of the ACS was Abraham Lincoln, a dyed-in-the-wool white separatist. Over time, he became literally obsessed with the idea of apartheid, which is one reason why, when he was a member of the Illinois legislature, he asked for funds to expel all free blacks from his state, or what he termed "the troublesome presence of the free negroes."³²³ This was also the reason he became a manager of the Illinois chapter of the national ACS³²⁴—at one time headed by the man he saw as the embodiment of human perfection,³²⁵ Henry Clay.³²⁶

We have seen that Lincoln was no abolitionist. But what is even less commonly known today is that he was a fiery white separatist, a black colonizationist, a supporter of American apartheid, and a powerful leader in the ACS, whose anti-black deportation agenda he once referred to (in the words of Clay) as "the benevolent efforts of the Colonization Society."³²⁷

If Abraham Lincoln is supposed to have been the "voice of American racial harmony," we are entitled to wonder why, on July 17, 1858, he made the following public statement during a speech at Springfield, Illinois:

☞ "What I would most desire would be the separation of the white and black races."³²⁸

Lincoln had many reasons for wanting to live apart from American blacks, or preferably, deport and colonize them. Being of a socialistic and racist mentality,³²⁹ one of the main reasons was his belief that whites should not have to compete for jobs with blacks, as he intimated in a September 17, 1859, speech at Cincinnati, Ohio:

☞ "... the mass of white men are really injured by the effects of slave-labor in the vicinity of the fields of their own labor . . ."[330]

Lincoln said much the same thing during his Cooper Union Speech on February 27, 1860:
☞ "Slavery is wrong in its effect upon white people and free labor. It is the only thing that threatens the Union."[331]

As noted, by far Lincoln's favorite person was big government Liberal, black colonizationist, and longtime slave owner Henry Clay of Kentucky, who passed away while serving as president of the American Colonization Society.[332] *At his first debate with Stephen A. Douglas on August 21, 1858, at Ottawa, Illinois, Lincoln referred to his racist icon as:*
☞ "Henry Clay, my beau ideal of a statesman, the man for whom I fought all my humble life."[333]

Such relationships only gave Lincoln's abolitionist critics more reasons to detest him. However, the Yankee president could have cared less how they felt. To all of them he repeatedly offered the same opinion regarding abolition and abolitionists, as he did when he gave the eulogy at Clay's funeral on July 16, 1852, in the State House at Springfield, Illinois:
☞ "Those who would shiver into fragments the Union of these States, tear to tatters its now venerated Constitution, and even burn the last copy of the Bible, rather than slavery should continue a single hour, together with all their more halting sympathizers, have received, and are receiving, their just execration; and the name and opinions and influence of Mr. Clay are fully and, as I trust, effectually and enduringly arrayed against them."[334]

During this same July 16 address, Lincoln went on to say:
☞ "The American Colonization Society was organized in 1816. Mr. Clay, though not its projector [that is, founder], was one of its earliest members; and he died, as for many preceding years he had been, its president. It was

one of the most cherished objects of his direct care and consideration, and the association of his name with it has probably been its very greatest collateral support. He considered it no demerit in the society that it tended, to relieve the slaveholders from *the troublesome presence of the free negroes*; but this was far from being its whole merit in his estimation. In the same speech from which we have quoted he [Clay] says:

> [Lincoln quoting Henry Clay] 'There is a moral fitness in the idea of returning to Africa her children, whose ancestors have been torn from her by the ruthless hand of fraud and violence. Transplanted in a foreign land, they will carry back to their native soil the rich fruits of religion, civilization, law, and liberty. May it not be one of the great designs of the Ruler of the universe, whose ways are often inscrutable by short-sighted mortals, thus to transform an original crime into a signal blessing to that most unfortunate portion of the globe?'

[Lincoln speaking his own words] "*This suggestion of the possible ultimate redemption of the African race and African continent was made twenty-five years ago. Every succeeding year has added strength to the hope of its realization. May it indeed be realized.* Pharaoh's country was cursed with plagues, and his hosts were lost in the Red Sea, for striving to retain a captive people who had already served them more than four hundred years. May like disasters never befall us! *If, as the friends of colonization hope, the present and coming generations of our countrymen shall by any means succeed in freeing our land from the dangerous presence of slavery, and at the same time in restoring a captive people to their long-lost fatherland* with bright prospects for the future, and this too so gradually that neither races nor individuals shall have suffered by the change, it will indeed be a *glorious consummation*. And if to such a consummation the efforts of Mr. Clay shall have contributed, it will be what he most ardently wished, and *none of his labors will have been more valuable to his country and his kind.*

"But Henry Clay is dead. His long and eventful life is closed. Our country is prosperous and powerful; but could it have been quite all it has been, and is, and is to be, without Henry Clay? Such a man the times have demanded, and such in the providence of God was given us. But he is gone. Let us strive to deserve, as far as mortals may, the continued care of Divine Providence, trusting that in future national emergencies He will not fail to provide us the instruments of safety and security [emphasis added]."[335]

Nine years on, now president of the United States, Lincoln was just as zealous about black colonization. In his "First Annual Message to Congress" on December 3, 1861, he once again took the opportunity to promote the idea of deporting blacks, in this case, free blacks. Lincoln here proposes to Congress that the U.S. "liberate" its slaves, purchase new foreign lands to put them on, then deport them there as soon as possible. As a result of this speech, in 1861 and 1862, Congress had $600,000 (about $15 million in today's currency) set aside to aid Lincoln's colonization proposal:[336]

☞ "Under and by virtue of the act of Congress entitled 'An act to confiscate property used for insurrectionary purposes,' approved August 6, 1861, the legal claims of certain persons to the labor and service of certain other persons have become forfeited; and numbers of the latter, thus liberated, are already dependent on the United States, and must be provided for in some way. Besides this, it is not impossible that some of the States will pass similar enactments for their own benefit respectively, and by operation of which persons of the same class will be thrown upon them for disposal. In such case I recommend that Congress provide for accepting such persons from such States, according to some mode of valuation, in lieu, *pro tanto* [that is, as far as it goes], of direct taxes, or upon some other plan to be agreed on with such States respectively; that such persons, on such acceptance by the General Government, be at once deemed free; and that, in any event, steps be taken for colonizing both classes (or the one first mentioned, if the other shall not be brought into existence) at some place or places in a climate congenial to them. It might be well to consider, too, whether the free colored people already in the United States could not, so far as individuals may desire, be included in such colonization.

"To carry out the plan of colonization may involve the acquiring of territory, and also the appropriation of money beyond that to be expended in the territorial acquisition. Having practised the acquisition of territory for nearly sixty years, the question of constitutional power to do so is no longer an open one with us. The power was questioned at first by Mr. [Thomas] Jefferson, who, however, in the purchase of Louisiana, yielded his scruples on the plea of great expediency. If it be said that the only legitimate object of acquiring territory is to furnish homes for white men, this measure effects that object; for the emigration of colored men leaves additional room for white men remaining or coming here. Mr. Jefferson, however, placed the importance of procuring Louisiana more on political and commercial grounds than on providing room for population.

"On this whole proposition, including the appropriation of money with the acquisition of territory, does not the expediency amount to absolute necessity—that without which the government itself cannot be perpetuated?"[337]

Five months later, on April 16, 1862, Lincoln helped push through the District of Columbia Emancipation Act, or as it was technically known: "An Act for the Release of Certain Persons held to Service or Labor in the District of Columbia." Both slaves and abolitionists rejoiced that anti-abolitionist Lincoln finally relented, banning slavery in the nation's capital. Up until then the president had been decidedly against shutting down America's largest slave mart,[338] *one located in full view of Northern members of Congress, who walked past it day after day without so much as wincing.*[339]

The shouts of joy and praise lasted only momentarily however. For when the entire act was read, abolitionists and black civil rights leaders were horrified to realize that it did not just call for the destruction of slavery in the District. It called for the immediate deportation of all those who were freed by the act as well. Lincoln had craftily worded the bill so that both the "friends of colonization," like himself, and abolitionists (who he abhorred) would benefit: the slaves would be liberated, then immediately sent out of the U.S. and settled in a foreign country, as he intimated in his April 16, "Message to Congress."[340] *Here is the exact wording of President Lincoln's Emancipation Proclamation for Washington, D.C.:*

☞ "An Act for the Release of certain Persons held to Service or Labor in the District of Columbia. "All persons held to service or labor within the District of Columbia by reason of African descent are hereby discharged and freed of and from all claim to such service or labor; and from and after the passage of this act neither slavery nor involuntary servitude, except for crime, whereof the party shall be duly convicted, shall hereafter exist in said District." All loyal persons holding claims against persons discharged by this act may, within 90 days from its passage, but not thereafter, present such claims in writing to the commissioners hereinafter mentioned. Three commissioners shall be appointed, residents of the District of Columbia, any two of whom shall have power to act, to investigate the validity and appraise and apportion the value in money of such claims; but the entire sum so appraised and apportioned shall not exceed in the aggregate an amount equal to $300 for each person shown to have been so held by lawful claim; and no claim shall be allowed for any slave or slaves brought into said District after the passage of this act, nor for any claimed by persons who have in any manner aided or sustained the rebellion against the Government of the United States. The commissioners shall within nine months deposit a full and final report of their proceedings and awards with the Secretary of the Treasury, who shall cause the amounts apportioned to be paid from the Treasury of the United States, except in the case of conflicting claims, in which 60 days are allowed for filing a bill in equity. $1,000,000 are appropriated for the purposes of this act, and $100,000 for the colonization of such free persons of African descent now residing in said District, or liberated by this act, as may desire to emigrate to the Republics of Hayti [Haiti] or Liberia, or such other country beyond the limits of the United States as the President may determine, at a rate not exceeding $100 for each emigrant."[341]

The same day a gloating President Lincoln sent a letter to the Senate and the House of Representatives concerning the District of Columbia Emancipation Act. It read, in part:
☞ "I am gratified that the two principles of compensation and colonization are both recognized and practically applied in the act."[342]

A few months later, on July 12, 1862, Lincoln addressed an "appeal" to representatives of the Border States concerning gradual and compensated emancipation. After spending several minutes explaining how his plan would help bring a speedy end to his War, he says:
☞ "Room in South America for colonization can be obtained cheaply and in abundance, and when numbers shall be large enough to be company and encouragement for one another, the freed people will not be so reluctant to go."[343]

Over time, Lincoln—arguably America's most famous and incorrigible white separatist—became more and more obsessed with the idea of American apartheid. During his an October 16, 1854, speech at Peoria, Illinois, and again on August 21, 1858, at Ottawa, Illinois, he publicly stated that, except for the many impracticalities involved, he would prefer to solve the "race problem" by shipping all American blacks back to Africa:

☞ "If all earthly power were given me, I should not know what to do, as to the existing institution. My first impulse would be to free all the slaves, and send them to Liberia [Africa],—to their own native land. But a moment's reflection would convince me, that whatever of high hope, (as I think there is) there may be in this, in the long run, its sudden execution is impossible. If they were all landed there in a day, they would all perish in the next ten days; and there are not surplus shipping and surplus money enough in the world to carry them there in many times ten days."[344]

On July 16, 1852, during his eulogy to Clay, Lincoln summed up the quintessential "problem" of slavery and emancipation in the following statement. According to our sixteenth president, for most Northern whites abolition was worse than slavery itself:
☞ "I think no wise man has perceived . . . how it [slavery] could be at once eradicated without producing a greater evil even to the cause of human liberty itself."[345]

In his "Second Annual Message to Congress" on December 1, 1862, Lincoln elaborated his position on the issue of black colonization. These thoughts were voiced just one month before he issued his Final Emancipation Proclamation on January 1, 1863:
☞ "Applications have been made to me by many free Americans of African descent to favor their emigration, with a view to such colonization as was contemplated in recent acts of Congress. Other parties at home and abroad—some from interested motives, others upon patriotic considerations, and still others influenced by philanthropic sentiments—have suggested similar measures; while, on the other hand, several of the Spanish-American republics have protested against the sending of such colonies to their respective territories. Under these circumstances, I have declined to move any such colony to any state without first obtaining the consent of its government, with an agreement on its part to receive and protect such emigrants in all the rights of freemen; and I have at the same time offered to the several states situated within the tropics, or having colonies there, to negotiate with them, subject to the advice and consent of the Senate, to favor the voluntary emigration of persons of that class to their respective territories, upon conditions which shall be equal, just, and humane. Liberia and Hayti [Haiti] are as yet the only countries to which colonists of African descent from here could go with certainty of being received and adopted as

citizens; and I regret to say such persons contemplating colonization do not seem so willing to migrate to those countries as to some others, nor so willing as I think their interest demands. I believe, however, opinion among them in this respect is improving; and that ere long there will be an augmented and considerable migration to both these countries from the United States."[346]

In order to ram his "white dream" of a black-free America[347] through Congress as quickly as possible, Lincoln had by now come up with his own black deportation plan, one based on a three-article amendment to the Constitution.[348] In this same annual message he outlines them as follows. The first article proposes compensating slave owners for the loss of their slaves if they emancipate them by the year 1900.[349] Importantly the second article states that all slaves liberated under this resolution will be "forever free."[350] Why is this important? The third article reveals the answer:

☞ "Congress may appropriate money and otherwise provide for colonizing free colored persons, with their own consent, at anyplace or places without the United States."[351]

Lincoln goes on to explain this particular clause in more detail:

☞ "The third article relates to the future of the freed people. It does not oblige, but merely authorizes, Congress to aid in colonizing such as may consent. This ought not to be regarded as objectionable, on the one hand or on the other, insomuch as it comes to nothing unless by the mutual consent of the people to be deported, and the American voters through their representatives in Congress. *I cannot make it better known than it already is, that I strongly favor colonization* [emphasis added]."[352]

The president then addresses the fears of white Northerners about the universal Yankee horror of a flood of freed Southern blacks migrating North, where they would allegedly compete with whites for jobs and intermingle with their sons and daughters. Again, the solution is colonization:

☞ "Is it true, then, that colored people can displace any more white labor by being free than by remaining slaves? If they stay in their old places, they jostle no white laborers; if they leave their old places, they leave them open to white laborers. Logically, there is neither more nor less of it.

Emancipation, even without deportation, would probably enhance the wages of white labor, and very surely would not reduce them. Thus, the customary amount of labor would still have to be performed; the freed people would surely not do more than their old proportion of it, and very probably for a time would do less, leaving an increased part to white laborers, bringing their labor into greater demand, and consequently enhancing the wages of it. With deportation, even to a limited extent, enhanced wages to white labor is mathematically certain. Labor is like any other commodity in the market—increase the demand for it, and you increase the price of it. Reduce the supply of black labor by colonizing the black laborer out of the country, and by precisely so much you increase the demand for, and wages of, white labor.

"But *it is dreaded that the freed people will swarm forth and cover the whole land?* Are they not already in the land? Will liberation make them any more numerous? Equally distributed among the whites of the whole country, and there would be but one colored to seven whites. Could the one in any way greatly disturb the seven? There are many communities now having more than one free colored person to seven whites, and this without any apparent consciousness of evil from it. The District of Columbia, and the States of Maryland and Delaware, are all in this condition. The District has more than one free colored to six whites; and yet in its frequent petitions to Congress I believe it has never presented the presence of free colored persons as one of its grievances. *But why should emancipation south send the free people north? People of any color seldom run unless there be something to run from.* Heretofore colored people, to some extent, have fled north from bondage; and now, perhaps, from both bondage and destitution. But *if gradual emancipation and deportation be adopted, they will have neither to flee from.* Their old masters will give them wages at least until new laborers can be procured; and *the freedmen, in turn, will gladly give their labor for the wages till new homes can be found for them in congenial climes and with people of their own blood and race. This proposition can be trusted on the mutual interests involved. And, in any event, cannot the North decide for itself whether to receive them?*

"Again, as practice proves more than theory, in any case, has there been any *irruption of colored people northward* because of the abolition of slavery in this District last spring [emphasis added]?"[353]

President Lincoln was so adamant about expatriating American blacks that he was willing to settle them almost anyplace—as long as it was, as he said, "without the United States."[354] Possible deportation sites included Africa, Europe, Latin America, and the Caribbean, or anywhere else they would be accepted. As such, he funded experimental colonies in what are now Panama and Belize, as well as in Haiti. All failed miserably, with death rates of over 50 percent in some cases.[355] The situation eventually became so horrendous that many of Lincoln's deported blacks begged to be allowed back into the U.S.

One of the more severe of these cases occurred on the Island of Vache, located off the coast of Haiti. On February 1, 1864, Lincoln was forced to deliver the following order to his secretary of war, Edwin M. Stanton. As an obviously disappointed Lincoln inadvertently admits here, over a year after issuing his bogus and unlawful Emancipation Proclamation, "freed" blacks in America's capital city still had not been welcomed by the president—or apparently by any other whites. Instead, all were relegated to the foul and seedy "camps for colored persons" then situated around Washington, D.C., just as the whites of Concord, Massachusetts, had done with their "freed" slaves only a few years earlier:[356]

☞ "Sir: You are directed to have a transport (either a steam or sailing vessel, as may be deemed proper by the Quartermaster-General) sent to the colored colony established by the United States at the Island of Vache, on the coast of San Domingo, to bring back to this country such of the colonists there as desire to return. You will have the transport furnished with suitable supplies for that purpose, and detail an officer of the Quartermaster's department, who, under special instructions to be given, shall have charge of the business. The colonists will be brought to Washington unless otherwise hereafter directed, and be employed and provided for at the camps for colored persons around that city. Those only will be brought from the island who desire to return, and their effects will be brought with them. Abraham Lincoln."[357]

On December 6, 1864, during his "Fourth Annual Message to Congress," President Lincoln brings up the ACS-created country of Liberia in Africa, one of his favorite topics; this time making reference to the many freed American blacks he had already sent there. In plain English, Lincoln says here that Liberia would grow in political power and population only as newly freed slaves were deported there from the U.S.:

☞ "Official correspondence has been freely opened with Liberia, and it gives us a pleasing view of social and political progress in that republic. It may be expected to derive new vigor from American influence, improved by the rapid disappearance of slavery in the United States."[358]

While strangely today's anti-South pro-Lincoln crowd refuses to acknowledge any of these well established facts, they have an even more difficult time accepting that our sixteenth president's unrelenting lobbying for colonization continued up until the very last day of his life. Actually, he never stopped thinking or talking about this subject.[359] *Indeed, there is no record of him ever renouncing his obsession with it.*[360]

Yet, for as long and as hard as he pitched his colonization program, it never officially made it past his Preliminary Emancipation Proclamation: Lincoln's cabinet removed all references to black deportation before he issued his final draft (on January 1, 1863)—the version best known to the public—because they feared it would alienate the Radicals in their party; that is, the abolitionists, whose votes would be needed in the president's 1864 reelection campaign.[361]

Let us now look at the pertinent portion of one our nation's most suppressed Yankee documents: Lincoln's Preliminary Emancipation Proclamation, issued on September 22, 1862. Why has it been kept in the shadows? As mentioned, it is because it contains part of Lincoln's black colonization plan:

☞ "Preliminary Emancipation Proclamation. By The President Of The United States Of America: I Abraham Lincoln, President of the United States of America, and commander-in-chief of the army and navy thereof, do hereby proclaim and declare . . . that it is my purpose, upon the next meeting of Congress, to again recommend the adoption of a practical measure tendering pecuniary aid to the free acceptance or rejection of all slave States, so called, the people whereof may not then be in rebellion against the United States, and which States may then have voluntarily adopted, or thereafter may voluntarily adopt, immediate or gradual abolishment of slavery within their respective limits; and that *the effort to colonize persons of African descent with their consent upon this continent or elsewhere, with the previously obtained consent of the governments existing there, will be continued.* . . . Abraham Lincoln [emphasis added]."[362]

On August 14, 1862, almost a year and a half into his war, Lincoln requested that a group of blacks meet with him at the White House. They were the first free African-Americans to ever enter those sacred halls. But due to our sixteenth president's deeply entrenched racism, it was not a gathering that Americans today would be proud of—which is why it has been relegated to the dust bin of history by pro-Lincoln scholars. I will now resuscitate it for all to see. *What follows is the complete conversation the "Great Emancipator" had with his stunned black guests, as recorded by Lincoln's personal friends and official biographers, John G. Nicolay and John Hay:*

☞ "[Nicolay and Hay speaking] Address On Colonization To A Deputation Of Colored Men. Washington, Thursday, August 14, 1862.

"This afternoon the President of the United States gave an audience to a committee of colored men at the White House. They were introduced by Rev. J. Mitchell, Commissioner of Emigration. E. M. Thomas, the chairman, remarked that they were there by invitation to hear what the Executive had to say to them.

"Having all been seated, the President, after a few preliminary observations, informed them that *a sum of money had been appropriated by Congress, and placed at his disposition, for the purpose of aiding the colonization in some country of the people, or a portion of them, of African descent, thereby making it his duty, as it had for a long time been his inclination, to favor that cause.* 'And why,' he asked, 'should the people of your race be colonized, and where? Why should they leave this country? This is, perhaps, the first question for proper consideration. *You and we are different races. We have between us a broader difference than exists between almost any other two races. Whether it is right or wrong I need not discuss; but this physical difference is a great disadvantage to us both, as I think. Your race suffer very greatly, many of them, by living among us, while ours suffer from your presence. In a word, we suffer on each side. If this is admitted, it affords a reason, at least, why we should be separated.* You here are freemen, I suppose?'

"A voice: 'Yes, sir.'

"The President: 'Perhaps you have long been free, or all your lives. Your race is suffering, in my judgment, the greatest wrong inflicted on any people. But even when you cease to be slaves, you are yet far removed from being placed on an equality with the white race. You are cut off from many of the advantages which the other race enjoys. The aspiration of men is to enjoy equality with the best when free, but on this broad continent not a single man of your race is made the equal of a single man of ours. Go where you are treated the best, and *the ban is still upon you.* I do not propose to discuss this, but to present it as a fact with which we have to deal. I cannot alter it if I would. It is a fact about which we all think and feel alike, I and you. We look to our condition. *Owing to the existence of the two races on this continent, I need not recount to you the effects upon white men, growing out of the institution of slavery.*

"'I believe in its general evil effects on the white race. See our present condition—the country engaged in war—our white men cutting one another's throats—none knowing how far it will extend—and then consider what we know to be the truth. But for your race among us there could not be war, *although many men engaged on either side do not care for you one way or the other*. Nevertheless, I repeat, without the institution of slavery, and the colored race as a basis, the war could not have an existence. *It is better for us both, therefore, to be separated.* I know that there are free men among you who, even if they could better their condition, are not as much inclined to go out of the country as those who, being slaves, could obtain their freedom on this condition. I suppose one of the principal difficulties in the way of colonization is that the free colored man cannot see that his comfort would be advanced by it. You may believe that you can live in Washington, or elsewhere in the United States, the remainder of your life as easily, perhaps more so, than you can in any foreign country; and hence *you may come to the conclusion that you have nothing to do with the idea of going to a foreign country.*

"'*This is (I speak in no unkind sense) an extremely selfish view of the case. You ought to do something to help those who are not so fortunate as yourselves.* There is an unwillingness on the part of our people, harsh as it may be, *for you free colored people to remain with us.* Now, if you could give a start to the white people, you would open a wide door for many to be made free. If we deal with those who are not free at the beginning, and whose intellects are clouded by slavery, we have very poor material to start with. *If intelligent colored men, such as are before me, would move in this matter, much might be accomplished.* It is exceedingly important that we have men at the beginning capable of thinking as white men, and not those who have been systematically oppressed. There is much to encourage you. For the sake of your race you should sacrifice something of your present comfort for the purpose of being as grand in that respect as the white people. It is a cheering thought throughout life, that something can be done to ameliorate the condition of those who have been subject to the hard usages of the world. It is difficult to make a man miserable while he feels he is worthy of himself and claims kindred to the great God who made him. In the American Revolutionary war sacrifices were made by men engaged in it, but they were cheered by the future. General Washington himself endured greater physical hardships than if he had remained a British subject, yet he was a happy man because he was engaged in benefiting his race, in doing something for the children of his neighbors, having none of his own.

"'*The colony of Liberia has been in existence a long time. In a certain sense it is a success.* The old President of Liberia, [Joseph Jenkins] Roberts, has just been with me—the first time I ever saw him. He says they have within the bounds of that colony between three and four hundred thousand people, or more than in some of our old States, such as Rhode Island or Delaware, or in some of our newer States, and less than in some of our larger ones. They are not all American colonists or their descendants. *Something less than 12,000 have been sent thither from this country. Many of the original settlers have died; yet, like people elsewhere, their offspring outnumber those deceased. The question is, if the colored people are persuaded to go anywhere, why not there?*

"'One reason for unwillingness to do so is that some of you would rather remain within reach of the country of your nativity. I do not know how much attachment you may have toward our race. It does not strike me that you have the greatest reason to love them. But still you are attached to them, at all events.

"'*The place I am thinking about for a colony is in Central America. It is nearer to us than Liberia—not much more than one fourth as far as Liberia, and within seven days' run by steamers. Unlike Liberia, it is a great line of travel—it is a highway. The country is a very excellent one for any people, and with great natural resources and advantages, and especially because of the similarity of climate with your native soil, thus being suited to your physical condition. The particular place I have in view is to be a great highway from the Atlantic or Caribbean Sea to the Pacific Ocean, and this particular place has all the advantages for a colony.* On both sides there are harbors—among the finest in the world. Again, there is evidence of very rich coal-mines. A certain amount of coal is valuable in any country. Why I attach so much importance to coal is, it will afford an opportunity to the inhabitants for immediate employment till they get ready to settle permanently in their homes. If you take colonists where there is no good landing, there is a bad show; and so where there is nothing to cultivate and of which to make a farm. But if something is started so that you can get your daily bread as soon as you reach there, it is a great advantage. Coal land is the best thing I know of with which to commence an enterprise.

"'To return—you have been talked to upon this subject, and told that a speculation is intended by gentlemen who have an interest in the country, including the coal-mines. We have been mistaken all our lives if we do not know whites, as well as blacks, look to their self-interest. Unless among those deficient of intellect, everybody you trade with makes something. You meet with these things here and everywhere. If such persons have what will be an advantage to them, the question is, whether it cannot be made of advantage to you? You are intelligent, and know that success does not so much depend on external help as on self-reliance. Much, therefore, depends upon yourselves. As to the coal-mines, I think I see the means available for your self-reliance. I shall, if I get a sufficient number of you engaged, have provision made that you shall not be wronged. *If you will engage in the enterprise, I will spend some of the money intrusted to me.* I am not sure you will succeed. The government may lose the money, but we cannot succeed unless we try; and we think, with care, we can succeed. The political affairs in Central America are not in quite as satisfactory a condition as I wish. There are contending factions in that quarter; but, it is true, all the factions are agreed alike on the subject of colonization, and want it, and are more generous than we are here.

"'To your colored race they have no objection. I would endeavor to have you made the equals, and have the best assurance that you should be, the equals of the best.

"'*The practical thing I want to ascertain is, whether I can get a number of able-bodied men, with their wives and children, who are willing to go when I present evidence of encouragement and protection. Could I get a hundred tolerably intelligent men, with their wives and children, and able to "cut their own fodder," so to speak? Can I have fifty? If I could find twenty-five able-bodied men, with a mixture of women and children,—good things in the family relation, I think,— I could make a successful commencement. I want you to let me know whether this can be done or not. This is the practical part of my wish to see you.* These are subjects of very great importance—worthy of a month's study, instead of a speech delivered in an hour. I ask you, then, to consider seriously, not pertaining to yourselves merely, nor for your race and ours for the present time, but as one of the things, if successfully managed, *for the good of mankind* . . . [end of Lincoln's dialogue].'

"The above is merely given as the substance of the President's remarks. The chairman of the delegation briefly replied that they would hold a consultation, and in a short time give an answer.

"The President said: 'Take your full time—no hurry at all.' The delegation then withdrew [emphasis added]."³⁶³

Lincoln's last comment was superfluous. *The five black delegates in attendance were in a state of humiliation, confusion, anger, and shock, and needed time to formulate a response.*

A few days later their reply arrived at the White House. The missive was brief and to the point. Furious, the black committee members scolded Lincoln for campaigning *for the deportation of America's colored people. They then asked him to please mind his own business!*[364]

When educated black leaders heard about Lincoln's disastrous "White House Conference" they were enraged. Easily seeing through the charade, Frederick Douglass, the prominent abolitionist, former Northern slave, and Lincoln's confidant, publicly denounced the president for his white racial arrogance, disdain for blacks, and rank dishonesty.[365] Furthermore, wrote a fuming Douglass in his newspaper:

> "The tone of frankness and benevolence which he assumes in his speech to the colored committee is too thin a mask not to be seen through. The genuine spark of humanity is missing in it. It expresses merely the desire to get rid of them . . ."[366]

Lincoln's March 12, 1864, "Message to the Senate" was devoted solely to the idea of exactly that: ridding the U.S. of its black inhabitants:

☞ "To the Senate of the United States: In obedience to the resolution of the Senate of the 28th of January last, I communicate herewith a report, with accompanying papers from the Secretary of the Interior, showing what portion of the appropriations for the colonization of persons of African descent has been expended, and the several steps which have been taken for the execution of the acts of Congress on that subject. Abraham Lincoln."[367]

As noted, Lincoln apologists and loyalists like to pretend that the president's racism and grotesque preoccupation with black colonization softened, and even disappeared, as time passed, particularly during his War. But this is not true. In fact, he was zealously discussing the issue right up until the day he died.

According to the memoirs of Yankee Union General Benjamin F. "the Beast" Butler (like Lincoln, also despised in the South for war crimes against humanity),[368] *in early April 1865 the president invited him to the White House to discuss his latest deportation plans to ship blacks out of the country.*[369] *This was just days before Lincoln was assassinated. Of his last meeting with Lincoln in April, Butler writes:*

☞ [Butler speaking] "A conversation was held between us after the negotiations had failed at Hampton Roads [a pointless and unsuccessful peace conference Lincoln had with several Confederate diplomats on February 3, 1865], and in the course of the conversation he said to me: —

"'But what shall we do with the negroes after they are free? I can hardly believe that the South and North can live in peace, unless we can get rid of the negroes. Certainly they cannot if we don't get rid of the negroes whom we have armed and disciplined and who have fought with us, to the amount, I believe of some one hundred and fifty thousand men. *I believe that it would be better to export them all to some fertile country with a good climate, which they could have to themselves.*

"'You have been a staunch friend of the race from the time you first advised me to enlist them at New Orleans. You have had a good deal of experience in moving bodies of men by water,—your movement up the James was a magnificent one. Now we shall have no use for our very large navy; *what, then, are our difficulties in sending all the blacks away?* [emphasis added]'"³⁷⁰

Lincoln was heartily disliked by many blacks during his presidency, in part because, as a manager in the American Colonization Society, he publicly announced his intention to ship all blacks "back to their native land." Black leader Frederick Douglass rightly called the president's ideas concerning African-Americans "racist," complaining that Lincoln himself was too full of white pride.

Butler responded by discussing his own idea of how to "send all the blacks away." The solution was simple: settle a colony for them in the Isthmus of Darien (modern Panama). Not knowing he would be dead in a few days, President Lincoln agreed, replying:

☞ "There is meat in that, General Butler; there is meat in that."³⁷¹

14

THE EMANCIPATION PROCLAMATION

FOR THE FIRST HALF OF his war (1861-1862), anti-abolitionist Lincoln cared little or nothing about freeing the slaves, and resisted all suggestions that he issue an emancipation proclamation. Because of this, angry abolitionists began calling him the "tortoise president," denouncing him at every opportunity,[372] even referring to him as "that damned idiot in the White House."[373]

When, under enormous pressure, he eventually issued his Final Emancipation Proclamation on January 1, 1863, it was not for the benefit of blacks, however. It was for the benefit of himself and other American whites, as is patently clear from the following quotes.

On September 13, 1862, here is how Lincoln replied "To A Committee From The Religious Denominations Of Chicago, Asking The President To Issue A Proclamation Of Emancipation." Lincoln's response should have been called "The Emancipation Proclamation: My Many Excuses for Blocking It and Delaying Its Issuance":

☞ "What good would a proclamation of emancipation from me do, especially as we are now situated? I do not want to issue a document that the whole world will see must necessarily be inoperative, like the Pope's bull against the comet. Would my word free the slaves, when I cannot even enforce the Constitution in the rebel States? Is there a single court, or magistrate, or individual that would be influenced by it there? And what reason is there to think it would have any greater effect upon the slaves than the late law of Congress, which I approved, and which offers protection and freedom to the slaves of rebel masters who come within our lines? Yet I cannot learn that that law has caused a single slave to come over to us. And suppose they could be induced by a proclamation of freedom from me to throw themselves upon us, what should we do with them? How can we feed and care for such a multitude?"[374]

Was the issuance of the Final Emancipation Proclamation legal? Plainly it was not. According to Lincoln's own wording, the edict was only active in the Confederacy,[375] *which had been a constitutionally formed independent nation for over two years by January 1, 1863. Thus he had no authority there, for the leader of one country cannot decide the laws of another. Because it violates both international law and the U.S. Constitution, this makes the military-based Emancipation Proclamation illegal, and its author, Abraham Lincoln, a war criminal. While not admitting he was a war criminal, Lincoln did openly confess that his proclamation was illicit.*[376] *In a September 2, 1863, letter to his secretary of the treasury, Salmon P. Chase, the president states that:*

☞ "The original proclamation has no constitutional or legal justification, except as a military measure."[377]

As we just saw above, on September 13, 1862, Lincoln told a group of abolitionist ministers that it was pointless to issue a proclamation of emancipation, for it would "necessarily be inoperative, like the Pope's bull against the comet."[378] *Why would it have been "inoperative"? Because it would have been rendered ineffective against the Constitution (the "comet"), making it unlawful.*

In his December 8, 1863, "Third Annual Message to Congress," Lincoln once again acknowledges the illegality of his proclamation, even admitting that it was only done as a "military measure":

☞ "According to our political system, as a matter of civil administration, the General Government had no lawful power to effect emancipation in any State, and for a long time it had been hoped that the rebellion could be suppressed without resorting to it as a military measure."[379]

Yankee and New South historians tell us that the Emancipation Proclamation enabled an egalitarian Lincoln to grant blacks full civil rights and incorporate them into American society. However, as we have seen, Lincoln was no egalitarian. More to the point, he issued his most famous edict for a number of reasons—not one of them having to do with black civil liberties.[380]

On February 6, 1864, for example, a year after his final proclamation was published, he hinted at the actual motivation behind it when he gave the following "Account of the Emancipation Proclamation" to artist Francis Bicknell Carpenter:

☞ "Things had gone from bad to worse until I felt that we had reached the end of our rope on the plan of operations we had been pursuing [that is, to quickly and efficiently crush the South]—that we had played our last card and must change our tactics, or lose the game. I determined on the Emancipation Proclamation, and . . . called a Cabinet meeting upon the subject. This was the last of July or the first part of the month of August, 1862 [author's note: the exact date was July 22, 1862]."[381]

Seeing the Civil War as little more than a tactical "card game," Lincoln always gave the same answer to the question of why he issued his famous edict: "military necessity." In fact, he often referred to his proclamation, never as a black civil rights emancipation, but as a "military emancipation," as he did to a group of Kentuckians on March 26, 1864:

☞ "When, early in the war, [Union] General [John C.] Fremont attempted military emancipation, I forbade it, because I did not then think it an *indispensable necessity*. When, a little later, [Union] General [Simon] Cameron, then Secretary of War, suggested the arming of the blacks, I objected because I did not yet think it an *indispensable necessity*. When, still later, [Union] General [David] Hunter attempted military emancipation, I again forbade it, because I did not yet think the *indispensable necessity* had come. When in March and May and July, 1862, I made earnest and successive appeals to the border States to favor compensated emancipation, I believed *the indispensable necessity for military emancipation and arming the blacks* would come unless averted by that measure. They declined the proposition, and I was, in my best judgment, driven to the alternative of either surrendering the Union, and with it the Constitution, or of *laying strong hand upon the colored element*. I chose the latter. In choosing it, I hoped for greater gain than loss; but of this, I was not entirely confident. More than a year of trial now shows no loss by it in our foreign relations, none in our home popular sentiment, none in *our white military force*—no loss by it anyhow or anywhere. On the contrary it shows a gain of quite a hundred and thirty thousand soldiers, seamen, and laborers. These are palpable facts, about which, as facts, there can be no caviling. *We have the men; and we could not have had them without the measure* [emphasis added]."³⁸²

Lincoln says here in no uncertain terms that he never considered emancipation until it became an "indispensable [military] necessity." Only then did he choose to "lay strong hand upon the colored element," and not one day before.

After years of refusing to issue an emancipation proclamation, Lincoln finally replied to his critics with this comment on September 16, 1862:

☞ "I view this matter as a practical war measure, to be decided on according to the advantages or disadvantages it may offer to the suppression of the rebellion."³⁸³

All doubt as to Lincoln's purpose for issuing the Emancipation Proclamation evaporates when we read the following, which the president wrote to Illinois politician James C. Conkling on August 26, 1863:

☞ "The war has certainly progressed as favorably for us since the issue of the proclamation as before. I know, as fully as one can know the opinions of others, that some of *the commanders of our armies in the field*, who have given us our most important successes, *believe the emancipation policy and the use of the colored troops constitute the heaviest blow yet dealt to the rebellion, and that at least one of these important successes could not have been achieved when it was but for the aid of black soldiers.* . . . You say you will not fight to free negroes. Some of them seem willing to fight for you; but no matter. Fight you, then, exclusively, to save the Union. *I issued the proclamation on purpose to aid you in saving the Union* [emphasis added]."³⁸⁴

---

*It was the very fact that he issued his proclamation purely out of "military necessity" that Lincoln had no organized plan to admit freed blacks into American society as equal citizens;*³⁸⁵ *nothing to help the elderly, the ill, or orphaned blacks who could not work and who had previously been under the lifelong care of their owners;*³⁸⁶ *no education, no loans or grants, no job training, no housing, to ease freedmen and freedwomen into the world of capitalism, competition, and a free, highly skilled, and often hostile labor force. Lincoln did not even offer them any legal protection.*³⁸⁷ *All were merely "liberated" to roam the streets and make their way as best they could. When asked how* the newly liberated freedmen and freedwomen were to survive, Lincoln compared them to feral hogs, replying flippantly:

☞ "Let them root, pig, or perish."³⁸⁸

Why did Lincoln consider his most famous document a "practical war measure," a "military necessity," or more plainly, a "military emancipation"? The answer is that he was running out of white soldiers due to disease, injuries, desertion, defection, and death, as he himself acknowledged.³⁸⁹ Incorrectly assuming that freed Southern blacks would automatically rush northward to join the Yankees, Lincoln also hoped to syphon off manpower from the Confederacy, which had been using blacks in their army and navy from the very first day of the Civil War,³⁹⁰ two years before Lincoln finally reluctantly allowed black enlistment.³⁹¹ Once, in the summer of 1864, when asked to defend his inhumane plan to free black slaves for the sole purpose of enlisting them in his armies, Lincoln gave this defensive but honest reply:

☞ ". . . no human power can subdue this rebellion without the use of the emancipation policy and every other policy calculated to weaken the moral and physical forces of the rebellion."³⁹²

Lincoln's problem was that slaves could not be made soldiers as long as they were considered "property."³⁹³ The resolution to this difficulty was the Emancipation Proclamation,³⁹⁴ which is why he later admitted that without his 200,000 additional black soldiers the North would not have won the war.³⁹⁵ Keep the "physical force" provided by the black Union soldier, said Lincoln on September 12, 1864,

☞ "and you can save the Union. Throw it away, and the Union goes with it."³⁹⁶

In my opinion the Emancipation Proclamation should have been entitled "The Proclamation to Officially Allow Black Enlistment in the Union Army," because—as this marked the North's official start of African-American enrollment³⁹⁷—this was its main purpose, as is clear from Lincoln's own wording in that document:

☞ "And by virtue of the power, and for the purpose aforesaid, I do order and declare that all persons held as slaves within said designated States and parts of States are, and henceforward forever shall be, free; and that the Executive Government of the United States, including the military and naval authorities thereof, will recognize and maintain the freedom of said persons."³⁹⁸

Far from being a civil rights document, Lincoln's Emancipation Proclamation also had a racist motivation behind it. As Lincoln later asserted on August 26, 1863:
☞ "I thought that whatever negroes could be got to do as soldiers, leaves just so much less for white soldiers to do in saving the Union."³⁹⁹

It was this need, to both replace lost white soldiers and relieve them of undesirable slave-like "grunt work," that prompted Lincoln to include the following clause near the end of his Final Emancipation Proclamation on January 1, 1863:
☞ "And I further declare and make known that such persons of suitable condition [that is, freed slaves] will be received into the armed service of the United States to garrison forts, positions, stations, and other places, and to man vessels of all sorts in said service."⁴⁰⁰

If there is any question left that Lincoln issued the Emancipation Proclamation primarily for military purposes, we need only carefully examine the wording of the following dispatch sent by the president to Yankee General Ulysses S. Grant on August 9, 1863:
☞ ". . . General [Lorenzo] Thomas has gone again to the Mississippi Valley, with the view of raising colored troops. I have no reason to doubt that you are doing what you reasonably can upon the same subject. I believe it [that is, the black soldier] is a resource which if vigorously applied now will soon close the contest. It works doubly, weakening the enemy and strengthening us. We were not fully ripe for it, until the river was opened. Now, I think at least one hundred thousand can and ought to be rapidly organized along its shores, relieving all white troops to serve elsewhere. Mr. [Charles Anderson] Dana understands you as believing that the emancipation proclamation has helped some in your military operations. I am very glad if this is so* [emphasis added]."⁴⁰¹

Following the issuance of his racist proclamation on January 1, 1863, Lincoln wasted no time in implementing its military aspects, as the following example illustrates. Written to Union General John Adams Dix on January 14, 1863, it reads:

☞ "My dear Sir: The proclamation has been issued. We were not succeeding—at best were progressing too slowly—without it. Now that we have it, and bear all the disadvantages of it (as we do bear some in certain quarters), we must also take some benefit from it, if practicable. I therefore will thank you for your well-considered opinion whether Fortress Monroe and Yorktown, one or both, could not, in whole or in part, be garrisoned by colored troops, leaving the white forces now necessary at those places to be employed elsewhere. Yours very truly, A. Lincoln."[402]

Shortly thereafter, Lincoln began desperately pushing for the formation of black U.S. troops, though up until then he had been completely against allowing African-Americans into the military, even as common slave-like laborers. On August 6, 1862, for instance, Lincoln's War Department sent the following brusque message to Edward Salomon, the governor of Wisconsin: "The President declines to receive Indians or negroes as troops."[403] Having finally changed his mind on the issue (though only after he had no choice), here is how he approached Tennessee's Governor Andrew Johnson on March 26, 1863, almost four months after issuing the Final Emancipation Proclamation:

☞ "My dear Sir: I am told you have at least thought of raising a negro military force. In my opinion the country now needs no specific thing so much as some man of your ability and position to go to this work. When I speak of your position, I mean that of an eminent citizen of a slave State and himself a slaveholder. *The colored population is the great available and yet unavailed of force for restoring the Union.* The bare sight of fifty thousand armed and drilled black soldiers upon the banks of the Mississippi would end the rebellion at once; and who doubts that we can present that sight if we but take hold in earnest? If you have been thinking of it, please do not dismiss the thought. Yours very truly, A. Lincoln [emphasis added]."[404]

Early evidence that Lincoln was thinking about freeing the slaves mainly for military purposes comes from September 13, 1862, the day he addressed a group of slavery-

hating clergymen who were trying to get the hesitant anti-abolitionist leader to issue an emancipation proclamation. Little wonder they were angry and frustrated: he had been stalling the process since the day he got into office, nearly two years earlier. Revealingly, none of the reasons Lincoln gives here for possibly freeing the slaves were for the benefit of blacks. Just as pathetic, he ends by intimating that he doubts African-Americans will be able to fight and handle their weapons properly, and that emancipation might not be a good idea because it could cause the white soldiers in the Border States to side with the Confederacy. All military issues! As the president phrased it, *I am not yet convinced that I should liberate the slaves, though if I did it must be admitted that*

☞ "... emancipation would help us in [attaining military support from] Europe, and convince them that we are incited by something more than ambition.[405] I grant, further, that it would help somewhat at the North [in maintaining support for the war], though not so much, I fear, as you and those you represent imagine. Still, some additional strength would be added in that way to the war, and then, unquestionably, it would weaken the rebels by drawing off their laborers, which is of great importance; but I am not so sure we could do much with the blacks. If we were to arm them, I fear that in a few weeks the arms would be in the hands of the rebels; and, indeed, thus far we have not had arms enough to equip our white troops. I will mention another thing, though it meet only your scorn and contempt. There are fifty thousand bayonets in the Union armies from the border slave States. It would be a serious matter if, in consequence of a proclamation such as you desire, they should go over to the rebels."[406]

In a private July 28, 1862, letter to Cuthbert Bullitt of New Orleans, Louisiana, Lincoln is completely transparent (for once) about why he issued the first draft of his Preliminary Emancipation Proclamation on July 22. Again, nothing about black civil rights here:

☞ "Mr. [Thomas J.] Durant complains that in various ways the relation of master and slave is disturbed by the presence of our army, and he considers it particularly vexatious that this, in part, is done under cover of an act of Congress, while constitutional guaranties are suspended on the plea of military necessity. The truth is, that *what is done and omitted about slaves is done and omitted on the same military necessity.* It is a military necessity to have men and money; and we can get neither in sufficient numbers or amounts if we keep from or drive from our lines slaves coming to them. Mr. Durant cannot

Lincoln stated unequivocally that if he could have saved the Union without freeing any slaves, he would have.

be ignorant of the pressure in this direction, nor of my efforts to hold it within bounds till he and such as he shall have time to help themselves [emphasis added]."⁴⁰⁷

———•••○•••———

*Shedding further light on the true motivations behind the Emancipation Proclamation is an exchange that took place between New York socialist and abolitionist Horace Greeley (a friend of Karl Marx) and Illinois anti-abolitionist Lincoln (idolized by Marx) in the summer of 1862.*⁴⁰⁸ *Greeley was one of Lincoln's greatest critics*⁴⁰⁹ *in a bitter contest that culminated on August 19 when the antislavery advocate published an open letter to the president in his newspaper, the* Tribune, *assaulting Lincoln's abysmal civil rights record and (absurdly) accusing him of prolonging the war by refusing to abolish slavery.*⁴¹⁰ *Here is Lincoln's reply four days later, on August 22, 1862:*

☞ "Dear Sir: I have just read yours of the 19ᵗʰ instant, addressed to myself through the New York *Tribune*. If there be in it any statements or assumptions of fact which I may know to be erroneous, I do not, now and here, controvert them. If there be any inferences which I may believe to be falsely drawn, I do not, now and here, argue against them. If there be perceptible in it an impatient dictatorial tone, I waive it in deference to an old friend whose heart I have always supposed to be right.

"As to the policy I 'seem to be pursuing,' as you say, I have not meant to leave any one in doubt.

"I would save the Union. I would save it in the shortest way under the Constitution. The sooner the national authority can be restored the nearer the Union will be 'the Union as it was.' *If there be those who would not save the Union unless they could at the same time save slavery, I do not agree with them. If there be those who would not save the Union unless they could at the same time destroy slavery, I do not agree with them. My paramount object is to save the Union, and not either to save or destroy slavery. If I could save the Union without freeing any slave, I would do it; and if I could save it by freeing all the slaves, I would do it; and if I could do it by freeing some and leaving others alone, I would also do that. What I do about slavery and the colored race, I do because I believe it helps to save this Union, and what I forbear, I forbear because I do not believe it would help to save the Union. I shall do less whenever I shall believe what I am doing hurts the cause, and I shall do more whenever I believe doing more will help the cause.* . . . Yours, A. Lincoln [emphasis added]."⁴¹¹

LINCOLN'S WAR ON THE SOUTH

WHILE DICTATORIAL LINCOLN WAS WAGING an illegal war on the seceded Southern states (a constitutionally formed republic), he was also simultaneously waging one on Southern states, such as Kentucky, that were not even full members of the Confederacy (only certain sections of the Bluegrass State had seceded). Here are some Lincoln quotes concerning Kentucky, as just one example, that one will never read in pro-North histories of the Civil War.

President Lincoln, consumed with his self-ordained authoritarian powers and completely ignoring the many constitutional limitations on the executive branch, illegally suspended habeas corpus *in one state after another throughout his War. One of his most bizarre proclamations in this regard came on July 5, 1864, when he slammed his iron fist down on his birth state, Kentucky, unnecessarily and unlawfully imposing martial law across the entire region:*

☞ "Whereas, by a proclamation which was issued on the fifteenth day of April, 1861, the President of the United States announced and declared that the laws of the United States had been for some time past, and then were, opposed, and the execution thereof obstructed, in certain States therein mentioned, by combinations too powerful to be suppressed by the ordinary course of judicial proceedings, or by the powers vested in the marshals by law;

"And whereas, immediately after the issuing of the said proclamation, the land and naval forces of the United States were put into activity to suppress the said insurrection and rebellion;

". . . And whereas many citizens of the State of Kentucky have joined the forces of the insurgents, and such insurgents have, on several occasions, entered the State of Kentucky in large force, and, not without aid and comfort furnished by disaffected and disloyal citizens of the United States residing therein, have not only disturbed the public peace, but have overborne the civil authorities and made flagrant civil war, destroying property and life in various parts of that State;

"And whereas it has been made known to the President of the United States by the officers commanding the national armies, that combinations have been formed in the said State of Kentucky with a purpose of inciting rebel forces to renew the said operations of civil war within the said State, and thereby to embarrass the United States armies now operating in the said States of Virginia and Georgia, and even to endanger their safety:

"Now, therefore, I, Abraham Lincoln, President of the United States, by virtue of the authority vested in me by the Constitution and laws, do hereby declare that, in my judgment, the public safety especially requires that the suspension of the privilege of the writ of *habeas corpus*,[412] so proclaimed in the said proclamation of the fifteenth of September, 1863, be made effectual and be duly enforced in and throughout the said State of Kentucky, and that martial law be for the present established therein. I do, therefore, hereby require of the military officers in the said State that the privilege of the writ of *habeas corpus* be effectually suspended within the said State according to the aforesaid proclamation, and that martial law be established therein, to take effect from the date of this proclamation, the said suspension and establishment of martial law to continue until this proclamation shall be revoked or modified, but not beyond the period when the said rebellion shall have been suppressed or come to an end. And I do hereby require and command, as well all military officers as all civil officers and authorities existing or found within the said State of Kentucky, to take notice of this proclamation, and to give full effect to the same.

"The martial law herein proclaimed, and the things in that respect herein ordered, will not be deemed or taken to interfere with the holding of lawful elections, or with the proceedings of the constitutional legislature of Kentucky . . . ."[413]

At the time Lincoln suspended *habeas corpus* it was illegal, for only Congress had this power. U.S. Chief Justice Roger B. Taney angrily ruled against Lincoln. Lincoln's response? He overturned the Constitution and had Taney arrested.

LINCOLN'S WAR ON THE NORTH

IT IS NOT COMMONLY KNOWN because the evidential material supporting the fact has been suppressed or ignored by pro-North historians, but Lincoln did not just wage war on the South and the Border States. Throughout his entire four years in the White House he also waged an unceasing assault on the Northern states. Using private vigilante gangs,[414] he illegally arrested and imprisoned tens of thousands of his constituents across the region, including not only everyday people, but newspaper editors, police officers, and even entire state legislatures, who did not support him or agree with him. Many languished in filthy Union prisons for the entire war.[415]

Lincoln deceptively based his unconstitutional crimes against his fellow Yankees on what he believed was or was not compatible with the "public interest." Actually, as is clear from his own words, it was only his megalomaniacal political ambitions that motivated him, not true justice.

On July 27, 1861, when confronted by the U.S. House of Representatives with a resolution asking him to explain why he was unlawfully arresting and imprisoning the police of Baltimore, Maryland, Lincoln refused to answer, instead giving this imperious reply:

☞ "In answer to the resolution of the House of Representatives of the 24th instant asking the grounds, reason, and evidence upon which the police commissioners of Baltimore were arrested and are now detained as prisoners at Fort McHenry, I have to state that it is judged to be incompatible with the public interest at this time to furnish the information called for by the resolution."[416]

Lincoln had no sympathy whatsoever for those Baltimore citizens he illegally arrested, illegally tried, and illegally jailed. One of these unfortunate souls was police officer John W. Davis, who refused to take Lincoln's equally illegal "Oath of Allegiance" to the U.S. government. Using the third person (as, oddly, he often did), here is how the tyrannical president (or one of his aids writing for him) replied to a protest against Davis' arrest on September 15, 1861. Let us note that only an autocrat like Lincoln could possibly believe that a citizen who refuses to pledge an unlawful oath to an authoritarian government is an "enemy" seeking to "destroy" that government!:

☞ "The President has read this letter, and he deeply commiserates the condition of any one so distressed as the writer seems to be. He does not know Mr. Davis—only knows him to be one of the arrested police commissioners of Baltimore because he says so in this letter. Assuming him to be one of those commissioners, the President understands Mr. Davis could at the time of his arrest, could at any time since, and can now, be released by taking a full oath of allegiance to the government of the United States, and that Mr. Davis has not been kept in ignorance of this condition of release. If Mr. Davis is still so hostile to the government, and so determined to aid its enemies in destroying it, he makes his own choice."[417]

In waging war on the Northern states, Lincoln violated both the Constitution and numerous state laws. He came close to admitting this when he stated, in so many words, that his "measures" might not be lawful. But he defended them anyway in his typically obscure manner, as he did on July 4, 1861, in his "Message to Congress in Special Session":

☞ "These measures, whether strictly legal or not, were ventured upon, under what appeared to be a popular demand and a public necessity; trusting then, as now, that Congress would readily ratify them."[418]

Besides illegally arresting and imprisoning tens of thousands of pro-peace and pro-South Northerners, most who had committed no crimes whatsoever, Lincoln also shut down between 300 and 400 Northern newspapers.[419] Why? For printing antiwar or anti-Lincoln articles. This Lincoln called "treason"! This is a total violation of the First Amendment, promising U.S. citizens freedom of speech.[420] But our Constitution-

loathing sixteenth president was not concerned with such matters, as can be seen in a May 18, 1864, letter he wrote to Union General John Adams Dix:

☞ "Whereas there has been wickedly and traitorously printed and published this morning in the New York *World* and New York *Journal of Commerce*, newspapers printed and published in the city of New York, a false and spurious proclamation, purporting to be signed by the President and to be countersigned by the Secretary of State, which publication is of a treasonable nature designed to give aid and comfort to the enemies of the United States and to the rebels now at war against the government, and their aiders and abettors: you are therefore hereby commanded forthwith to arrest and imprison, in any fort or military prison in your command, the editors, proprietors, and publishers of the aforesaid newspapers, and all such persons as, after public notice has been given of the falsehood of said publication, print and publish the same with intent to give aid and comfort to the enemy; and you will hold the persons so arrested in close custody until they can be brought to trial before a military commission for their offense. You will also take possession, by military force, of the printing establishments of the New York *World* and *Journal of Commerce*, and hold the same until further orders, and prevent any further publication therefrom."[421]

Lincoln's many crimes against both the Constitution and the American people are still being counted and studied by objective scholars. The exact number and scale have yet to be determined.

Lincoln's ridiculous, unnecessary, and illicit arrest and deportation of the well liked Conservative Ohio Congressman Clement Laird Vallandigham—for spreading pro-peace sentiment—understandably outraged the president's Northern constituents. As always, Lincoln justified his crime with equally ludicrous reasoning, as can be seen in a June 12, 1863, letter he wrote to New Yorker Erastus Corning:

☞ "[Vallandigham] was not arrested because he was damaging the political prospects of the administration or the personal interests of the commanding general, but because he was damaging the army, upon the existence and vigor of which the life of the nation depends. He was warring upon the military, and this gave the military constitutional jurisdiction to lay hands upon him."[422]

LINCOLN'S WAR CRIMES

AS WE WILL SEE IN this chapter, Lincoln overturned the Constitution, ignoring those clauses he did not like while reinterpreting the rest to suit his personal ambitions. While many presidents (Liberal and Conservative) have often overstepped their small circle of limited powers (as set out in Article 4, Section 4) in just this way,[423] none took it to such extremes as Lincoln. In the wake of his war on the Constitution, Lincoln perpetuated a litany of crimes so massive that historians and Lincoln scholars are still busy studying and counting them all.

For example, "Honest Abe" did far more than just illegally shut down as many as 400 Northern newspapers,[424] confiscate their presses, and jail their owners,[425] suspend *habeas corpus* for the first time across the entire U.S.,[426] and unlawfully arrest and imprison tens of thousands of law abiding Northern citizens,[427] he was also the first and only president in U.S. history to order a mass execution of his own citizens (in this case, a group of Native-Americans, angry over the federal government's many broken promises and treaties).[428]

Lincoln also illegally seized rail and telegraph lines leading to the capital;[429] used spies, detectives, "secret agents,"[430] fraud, and bribery to insure his reelection in 1864—resulting in "the foulest corruptions" (said to have been obvious at every level of his party);[431] unlawfully ordered a naval blockade of Southern ports;[432] "checked" (arrested) clergymen who had "become dangerous to the public interest" (that is, who contradicted Lincoln);[433] intimidated judges;[434] closed the post office in an effort to prevent anti-Lincoln, antiwar mail from being sent or delivered;[435] forced all federal employees to contribute 5 percent of their annual income to his 1864 re-election campaign;[436] defied the U.S. Supreme Court;[437] used the U.S. military to prevent Northern state legislatures from meeting;[438] shut down the governments of entire Northern states and arrested members of their state legislatures;[439] levied the first personal income tax (launching what would later become the Internal Revenue Service, or IRS);[440] prevented governmental debate over secession;[441] illegally created the state of West Virginia from the state of Virginia;[442] rigged Northern elections to skew the outcome in his favor;[443] intimidated and bribed voters, soldiers, and fellow politicians to vote for his party;[444] had blacks who refused to enlist in his army whipped or even shot to death;[445] and even tortured both Northern soldiers (accused of desertion) and Northern citizens (accused of espousing antiwar sentiment).[446] And this was just for starters!

How was he able to get away with such outrages?

The answer comes from his imagined theory known as "military necessity,"[447] which he wrongly believed could be activated by the president during times of "rebellion." We have seen, however, that the South was not in "rebellion." She had no desire to attack the U.S., take its land, or conquer its people. She merely wanted to be "let alone" to form her own republic,[448] which she had every right to do under the Ninth and Tenth Amendments.[449]

Lincoln's belief in the idea of military necessity gave him unfettered freedom to do whatever he pleased, particularly regarding the Constitution, an inherently conservative document that clearly irritated the big government Liberal. As he said in a letter to one of his Yankee generals on August 9, 1864:

☞ "Nothing justifies the suspending of the civil by the military authority, but military necessity . . ."[450]

Lincoln's war on the South, in turn, gave him full justification for using military necessity any time he chose, since he believed—as we have seen—that everything, including the Emancipation Proclamation, was related to the military.[451] As he said on July 28, 1862:

☞ "The truth is, that what is done and omitted about slaves is done and omitted on the same military necessity. It is a military necessity to have men and money; and we can get neither in sufficient numbers or amounts if we keep from or drive from our lines slaves coming to them."[452]

One odious example of Lincoln's use of "military necessity" was his brazen violation of what would become the internationally recognized Geneva Conventions. According to a private September 22, 1861, letter Lincoln wrote to Orville Hickman Browning:
☞ "If a commanding general finds a necessity to seize the farm of a private owner for a pasture, an encampment, or a fortification, he has the right to do so, and to so hold it as long as the necessity lasts; and this is within military law, because within military necessity."[453]

In an August 9, 1864, letter to one of his military officers, Lincoln discards all self-restraint and regard for the Constitution, saying:
☞ "I now think you would better place whatever you feel is necessary to be done on this distinct ground of military necessity . . ."[454]

Such outrageous pronouncements, of course, opened the door for nearly unlimited corruption and abuses by Lincoln's soldiers. For once this door was unlocked, many of them, like Yankee war criminals Ulysses S. Grant, William T. Sherman, and Philip H. Sheridan, gladly walked right through it and never looked back. Lincoln, of course, never admitted to any of his war crimes, or those of his soldiers. However, we can detect hints of what some of these were from his letters and dispatches. One particularly troublesome Yank officer was Benjamin F. "the Beast" Butler, widely known for his vile depredations upon the Southern people. Lincoln acknowledged the fact in an understated January 19, 1865, letter to his secretary of war, Edwin M. Stanton:
☞ "Dear Sir: You remember that from time to time appeals have been made to us by persons claiming to have attempted to come through our lines with their effects to take the benefit of the amnesty proclamation, and to have been despoiled of their effects under General Butler's administration. Some of these claims have color of merit, and may be really meritorious. Please consider whether we cannot set on foot an investigation which may advance justice in the premises. Yours truly, A. Lincoln."[455]

Yankee slave owner and colonizationist General Ulysses S. Grant[456] received a telegram from Lincoln regarding the crimes of Union soldiers. Dated August 14, 1864, it reads:

☞ "The Secretary of War and I concur that you had better confer with General [Robert E.] Lee, and stipulate for a mutual discontinuance of house-burning and other destruction of private property. The time and manner of conference and particulars of stipulation we leave, on our part, to your convenience and judgment. A. Lincoln."⁴⁵⁷

On April 4, 1864, Lincoln tried to justify his staggering criminal, bigoted, and anti-American activities with the following bizarre declaration, sounding more like a delusional dictator than a U.S. president:

☞ "I felt that measures otherwise unconstitutional might become lawful by becoming indispensable to the preservation of the Constitution through the preservation of the nation. Right or wrong, I assumed this ground and I now avow it."⁴⁵⁸

Lincoln at Antietam, Maryland, with some of his officers in the fall of 1862. One of the president's greatest critics, Yankee General George B. McClellan—who likened Lincoln to something between a baboon and a gorilla—stands second from left facing his boss.

RELIGION

THOUGH LINCOLN LIKED TO PASS himself off as a "good Christian," he was actually a skeptic, a humanist, and—as his friends and family knew him—an "infidel," one who opposed organized religion, told impious stories,[459] denounced his wife's spiritualism,[460] never prayed, never attended church, never joined any religious faith or denomination,[461] never opened a Bible, never mentioned Jesus, and was well-known for his lack of belief in the divinity of Christ, Christian salvation, the sanctity of the Bible, and even in God himself. Lincoln even once declared Jesus a "bastard" while asserting that the Bible's miracles went against the laws of Nature.[462] In fact, our sixteenth president, who often criticized fellow politicians for mixing theology and politics, and who enjoyed arguing against the Bible in public,[463] much preferred reading the works of atheists like Thomas Paine and Voltaire over the works of religionists.[464]

Lincoln once authored an essay demonstrating that, far from being inspired, the Bible was actually "uninspired" and historically inaccurate,[465] and in Illinois in the mid 1830s he wrote "a little book on infidelity," defending atheism and criticizing Christianity.[466] Lincoln was saved from eternal disgrace by Samuel Hill, his employer at the time, who—knowing it would certainly ruin the author's future—ripped the manuscript from young Abe's hands and hurled it into a burning stove.[467] If this book had survived we can be sure that Lincoln would not be worshiped as the Christ-like canonized figure he is today!

Here is what William H. Herndon—one of Lincoln's closest friends, business associates, and biographers—wrote on the subject:

> "Lincoln was a deep-grounded infidel. He disliked and despised churches. He never entered a church except to scoff and ridicule. On coming from a church he would mimic the preacher. Before running for any office, he wrote a book against Christianity and the Bible. He showed it to some of his friends and read extracts. A man named Hill was greatly shocked and urged Lincoln not to publish it; urged it would kill him politically. Hill got this book in his

hands, opened the stove door, and it went up in flames and ashes. After that Lincoln became more discreet, and when running for office often used words and phrases to make it appear that he was a Christian. He never changed on this subject; he lived and died a deep-grounded infidel."[468]

Lincoln's rank atheism and scurrilous anti-Christian views have been thoroughly suppressed by pro-Lincoln historians. Yet, some vestiges remain, as this chapter illustrates.

An interesting incident in Lincoln's pre-presidential life sheds light on his so-called "faith." One Sunday, while he was a candidate for Congress, he showed up in church, no doubt to canvass for votes. At one point in his sermon the minister said to the congregation: "All who wish to go to Heaven, please stand up." Everyone in the chapel promptly got to their feet, except one: Abraham Lincoln. The surprised clergyman turned to the towering ill-dressed rustic and asked: "Mr. Lincoln, where do you wish to go?" "I wish to go to Congress," he replied snidely.[469] *Regular churchgoers were not amused. And neither was the local clergy. Twenty out of the twenty-three ministers, as well as "a very large majority" of the prominent members of the churches in his hometown of Springfield, Illinois, later opposed him for president.*[470]

Lincoln was so hostile toward religion, and in particular Christianity, and so arrogantly intolerant of preachers, priests, and evangelists, that he did not trust himself to be in their presence for fear of making a public spectacle. He provided plenty of ammunition for his critics on this topic, such as the admission he made in a May 7, 1837, letter to Mary Owens in which he said:

☞ "I've never been to church yet, nor probably shall not be soon. I stay away because I am conscious I should not know how to behave myself."[471]

Lincoln's own remarks have condemned him for all time as an atheist, or at the very least, a non-believing skeptic and agnostic. He was certainly not a follower of the Prince of Peace. He once flatly told Newton Bateman, the Superintendent of Public Instruction for the state of Illinois:

☞ "I am not a Christian."[472]

Once, when Lincoln was considering fighting a duel with James A. Shields, his friends intervened saying that such violence was against the Bible and the teachings of Jesus. Lincoln snapped back:
☞ "The Bible is not my book, nor Christianity my profession."[473]

As late as 1862 Lincoln was still openly denouncing religion, and in particular Christianity. That year a man named Judge Wakefield wrote Lincoln, inquiring as to whether he had accepted Christianity yet, to which the Yankee president replied:
☞ "My earlier views of the unsoundness of the Christian scheme of salvation and the human origin of the scriptures have become clearer and stronger with advancing years and I see no reason for thinking I shall ever change them."[474]

Around the same time, Manford's Magazine *quoted Lincoln as saying:*
☞ "It will not do to investigate the subject of religion too closely, as it is apt to lead to Infidelity [atheism]."[475]

As a typical tyrannical Liberal who detested traditional Christianity, it is only fitting that the Lincoln Memorial in Washington, D.C. was designed as a Pagan "temple" and that Lincoln's statue was based on the ancient Greek god Zeus sitting imperiously on his throne. (Note the engraved words.)

QUOTABLE QUOTES ABOUT LINCOLN

They Don't Want You To Know!

"The president is nothing more than a well meaning baboon. He is the original gorilla. What a specimen to be at the head of our affairs now!"[476] — GEORGE B. MCCLELLAN, Union general

"The man who could open a Cabinet meeting called to discuss the Emancipation Proclamation by reading Artemus Ward,[477] who called for a comic song on the bloody battle-field,[478] was the same man who could guide with clear mind and iron hand the diplomacy that kept off the fatal interference of Europe, while conducting at home the most horrible of all civil wars that ever afflicted a people. He reached with ease the highest and the lowest level, and on the very field that he shamed with a ribald song he left a record of eloquence never reached by human lips before."[479] — DONN PIATT, Union general

"Thus has it been with Mr. Lincoln—a weak and imbecile man; the weakest man that I ever knew in a high place; for I have seen him and conversed with him, and I say here, in my place in the Senate of the United States, that I never did see or converse with so weak and imbecile a man as Abraham Lincoln, President of the United States. . . . if I wanted to paint a tyrant, if I wanted to paint a despot, a man perfectly regardless of every constitutional right of the people, who's sworn servant, not ruler, he is, I would paint the hideous form of Abraham Lincoln."[480] — WILLARD SAULSBURY, Yankee senator

"The President, his advisers, his commanding generals . . . whose shaping hands have had so much to do with the conduct of the war, must all of them be weighed in the balance by the people and the generations to come. 'The great soul of the world is just,' and sooner or later all disguises will be thrown off, and every historical character will stand forth as he is, in the light of his deeds and deserts. . . . Justice will be done; but that justice may brand as a crime the blunders proceeding from a feeble, timid, ambidextrous policy, resulting in great sacrifices of life and treasure, and periling the priceless interests at stake."[481] — GEORGE W. JULIAN, Northern Congressman under Lincoln

"As to Mr. Lincoln's religious views he was, in short, an infidel . . . He did not believe that Jesus was God, nor the Son of God,—[he] was a fatalist, denied the freedom of the will. Mr. Lincoln told me *a thousand times* that he did not believe the Bible was the revelation of God, as the Christian world contends."[482] — WILLIAM H. HERNDON, Lincoln's law partner and friend

"We charge, and without the fear of successful contradiction, that Mr. Lincoln, as the head of the Federal Government, and the Commander-in-Chief of its armies, was directly responsible for the outrages committed by his subordinates; and that the future and unprejudiced historian will so hold him responsible. . . . Will the people of the South lick the hand that thus smote their fathers, their mothers, their brethren and their sisters by now singing paeans of glory to his name and fame?"[483] — GEORGE L. CHRISTIAN, Confederate officer and Virginia judge

"The most striking thing is the absence of personal loyalty to the President. It does not exist. He has no admirers. If a convention were held tomorrow he would not get the vote of a single state."[484] — RICHARD H. DANA, Yankee abolitionist

"Lincoln is, to the extent of his limited ability and narrow intelligence, the [Liberal party's] willing instrument for all the woe which [has] thus far been brought upon the country and for all the degradation, all the atrocity, all the desolation and ruin."[485] — FRANKLIN PIERCE, U.S. president

On September 6, 1864, the New York *Daily Tribune* noted that Lincoln had been called the following names by his Northern political associates, many of them from his own party: "filthy story-teller," "despot," "liar," "thief," "buffoon," "usurper," "monster," "Ignoramus Abe," "old scoundrel," "perjurer," "swindler," "tyrant," "fiend," and "butcher."[486] For his anti-abolitionist stance and great reluctance to free the slaves, Lincoln was termed America's "largest slave holder" by Boston abolitionist Charles Sumner.[487]

NOTES

1. Nicolay and Hay, ALCW, Vol. 1, p. 431.
2. Nicolay and Hay, ALCW, Vol. 1, p. 259.
3. Nicolay and Hay, ALCW, Vol. 1, p. 369.
4. Nicolay and Hay, ALCW, Vol. 1, p. 15. See also p. 642.
5. *Southern Review*, January 1873, Vol. 12, No. 25, p. 364.
6. Current, LNK, p. 58.
7. Remsburg, pp. 220-221.
8. For a detailed discussion of this topic, see Seabrook, ALWALJDWAC.
9. Neely, p. 53.
10. A. Cooke, ACA, p. 216.
11. *U.S. Grant: Warrior*, PBS, January 10, 2011.
12. See e.g., Oates, AL, p. 17.
13. See e.g., Tagg, passim.
14. J. Davis, RFCG, Vol. 1, p. 62.
15. Gordon, p. 111.
16. Nicolay and Hay, ALCW, Vol. 2, p. 296.
17. Nicolay and Hay, ALAH, Vol. 10, p. 123. See also DiLorenzo, LU, p. 25.
18. Seabrook, AL (hardcover ed.), pp. 6, 373-374, 479.
19. Seabrook, L, pp. 404-407.
20. Seabrook, EYWTACWW, p. 95.
21. Seabrook, EYWTACWW, pp. 116-131, 146-56.
22. Nicolay and Hay, ALCW, Vol. 1, p. 355.
23. Seabrook, L, p. 13.
24. Seabrook, L, pp. 921-925.
25. Seabrook, L, pp. 13-14.
26. Nicolay and Hay, ALCW, Vol. 1, p. 533. Lincoln said the same thing to Samuel Galloway in a July 28, 1859, letter. Nicolay and Hay, ALCW, Vol. 1, p. 538.
27. Villard, Vol. 1, p. 96.
28. Nicolay and Hay, ALCW, Vol. 1, p. 522.
29. Meriwether, p. 9.
30. Nicolay and Hay, ALCW, Vol. 1, p. 634.
31. Nicolay and Hay, ALCW, Vol. 2, pp. 531-532.
32. Nicolay and Hay, ALCW, Vol. 1, p. 684.
33. Nicolay and Hay, ALCW, Vol. 1, p. 685.
34. Nicolay and Hay, ALCW, Vol. 1, p. 687.
35. Nicolay and Hay, ALCW, Vol. 1, p. 19.
36. Lamon, RAL, pp. 189-190.
37. Nicolay and Hay, ALCW, Vol. 2, p. 484.
38. Nicolay and Hay, ALCW, Vol. 1, p. 677.
39. Nicolay and Hay, ALCW, Vol. 1, p. 678.
40. *House Documents*, p. 91. See also Nicolay and Hay, ALCW, Vol. 2, p. 509.
41. Mitgang, pp. 8-12, 205.
42. Nicolay and Hay, ALCW, Vol. 1, p. 298. See also p. 422.
43. See Findlay and Findlay, pp. 168-169, 212-217.
44. Nicolay and Hay, ALCW, Vol. 1, p. 225.
45. Nicolay and Hay, ALCW, Vol. 2, p. 615.
46. Nicolay and Hay, ALCW, Vol. 2, p. 440.
47. Nicolay and Hay, ALCW, Vol. 1, p. 226.
48. Nicolay and Hay, ALCW, Vol. 2, p. 53.
49. Nicolay and Hay, ALCW, Vol. 1, p. 574.
50. Findlay and Findlay, pp. 168-169, 212-217.
51. Nicolay and Hay, ALCW, Vol. 1, p. 178.
52. Nicolay and Hay, ALCW, Vol. 1, p. 129.
53. See Findlay and Findlay, pp. 20-23.
54. Nicolay and Hay, ALCW, Vol. 1, p. 198.
55. Nicolay and Hay, ALCW, Vol. 1, p. 635.
56. Nicolay and Hay, ALCW, Vol. 1, p. 229.
57. Nicolay and Hay, ALCW, Vol. 1, p. 359.
58. Coffin, p. 235. Lincoln devotee President Barack Hussein Obama recently made a similar statement, calling the U.S. Constitution "an imperfect document." "Glenn Beck," FOX News, September, 17, 2009 (Constitution Day, 222nd anniversary).

59. Nicolay and Hay, ALCW, Vol. 1, p. 691.
60. The presidential oath is taken in accordance with Article 2, Section 1, Clause 8 of the U.S. Constitution. Findlay and Findlay, p. 124.
61. For a detailed examination of this topic, see Seabrook, AWAITBLA. For more on the history and legality of secession in the U.S. pertaining specifically to Lincoln, see Seabrook, AL, pp. 81-102.
62. Nicolay and Hay, ALCW, Vol. 1, p. 105.
63. Nicolay and Hay, ALCW, Vol. 1, p. 138.
64. Nicolay and Hay, ALCW, Vol. 1, p. 195.
65. Nicolay and Hay, ALCW, Vol. 1, pp. 253-254.
66. Nicolay and Hay, ALCW, Vol. 1, p. 425.
67. Nicolay and Hay, ALCW, Vol. 1, p. 533.
68. Nicolay and Hay, ALCW, Vol. 1, p. 534.
69. Nicolay and Hay, ALCW, Vol. 1, pp. 661-662.
70. Nicolay and Hay, ALCW, Vol. 1, pp. 4-5.
71. Nicolay and Hay, ALCW, Vol. 2, p. 61.
72. Nicolay and Hay, ALCW, Vol. 2, p. 437.
73. Nicolay and Hay, ALCW, Vol. 2, p. 63.
74. Nicolay and Hay, ALCW, Vol. 1, p. 63.
75. Nicolay and Hay, ALCW, Vol. 1, p. 63.
76. Seabrook, TMCP, p. 469.
77. Findlay and Findlay, pp. 212-217.
78. Seabrook, TMCP, pp. 240-241.
79. Nicolay and Hay, ALCW, Vol. 2, pp. 61-62.
80. Pollard, LC, p. 175.
81. Here in the South we shun the term "Civil War," and for good reason. Seabrook, EYWTACWW, pp. 25-27.
82. See Seabrook, LW, passim. Also see Seabrook, EYWTACWW, pp. 40-47.
83. Nicolay and Hay, ALCW, Vol. 2, p. 1.
84. Nicolay and Hay, ALCW, Vol. 1, pp. 420-421.
85. Nicolay and Hay, ALCW, Vol. 1, p. 427.
86. Nicolay and Hay, ALCW, Vol. 2, pp. 512-513.
87. Nicolay and Hay, ALCW, Vol. 2, pp. 651-652.
88. Nicolay and Hay, ALCW, Vol. 2, pp. 575-576.
89. Nicolay and Hay, ALCW, Vol. 2, p. 562.
90. Nicolay and Hay, ALCW, Vol. 2, p. 271.
91. Nicolay and Hay, ALCW, Vol. 2, p. 657.
92. Nicolay and Hay, ALAH, Vol. 4, p. 76. Little wonder that one of Lincoln's political rivals, Illinois Senator Stephen A. Douglas, once said of Lincoln: "He has a fertile genius in devising language to conceal his thoughts. . . . Lincoln is to be voted in the south as a proslavery man, and he is to be voted for in the north as an Abolitionist . . . [for] he can trim his principles any way in any section, so as to secure votes." Nicolay and Hay, ALCW, Vol. 1, pp. 468, 433, 451.
93. Nicolay and Hay, ALCW, Vol. 1, p. 240.
94. Hayden, pp. 545-546.
95. Christian, p. 14; Hayden, p. 546.
96. Nicolay and Hay, ALCW, Vol. 2, p. 358.
97. Nicolay and Hay, ALCW, Vol. 2, p. 674.
98. Nicolay and Hay, ALCW, Vol. 2, p. 534.
99. See Seabrook, EYWTACWW, pp. 40-47.
100. Lester, pp. 359-360.
101. Nicolay and Hay, ALCW, Vol. 1, p. 347.
102. Seabrook, EYWTACWW, pp. 88-89.
103. See Findlay and Findlay, p. 164.
104. Nicolay and Hay, ALCW, Vol. 1, p. 176.
105. Nicolay and Hay, ALCW, Vol. 1, p. 187.
106. C. Adams, p. 135; DiLorenzo, GC, p. 255; Johannsen, p. 55.
107. Nicolay and Hay, ALCW, Vol. 1, p. 659.
108. Seabrook, ARB, pp. 48-49.
109. Nicolay and Hay, ALCW, Vol. 1, p. 609.
110. D. H. Donald, L, p. 363; Leech, p. 155.
111. Quarles, NCW, pp. 115-116.
112. Leech, p. 151; Black, p. 165. Lincoln later stripped Frémont of his command for freeing slaves in his assigned military area. K. C. Davis, p. 439.
113. Quarles, pp. 113-114.
114. Black, p. 165; Wiley, SN, pp. 296-298; Leech, pp. 305-306.

115. Lincoln admitted that he nullified the emancipation proclamations of these men because, as he put it, there was no "indispensable necessity." Nicolay and Hay, ALCW, Vol. 2, p. 508. The nation's 4.5 million slaves (1 million in the North and 3.5 million in the South) at the time must have wondered what he meant by this.
116. Nicolay and Hay, ALCW, Vol. 2, p. 154.
117. Nicolay and Hay, ALCW, Vol. 2, p. 155.
118. Nicolay and Hay, ALCW, Vol. 2, p. 77.
119. Nicolay and Hay, ALCW, Vol. 2, pp. 80-81.
120. Lincoln and Douglas, p. 268.
121. Litwack, NS, p. 276.
122. Nicolay and Hay, ALCW, Vol. 1, p. 15. See also p. 642.
123. Nicolay and Hay, ALCW, Vol. 1, p. 174.
124. For a full discussion on the origins of 19th-Century Republican Party (which has no connection to today's Republican Party), see Seabrook, ALWALJDWAC.
125. Nicolay and Hay, ALCW, Vol. 1, p. 349.
126. McKissack and McKissack, pp. 134, 135.
127. See e.g., Nicolay and Hay, ALCW, Vol. 2, p. 357.
128. W. Phillips, p. 456.
129. See e.g., Nicolay and Hay, ALCW, Vol. 2, p. 365.
130. Nicolay and Hay, ALCW, Vol. 2, p. 205.
131. Nicolay and Hay, ALCW, Vol. 2, p. 296.
132. Nicolay and Hay, CWAL, Vol. 1, p. 275.
133. Nicolay and Hay, CWAL, Vol. 1, pp. 275-276.
134. Nicolay and Hay, ALCW, Vol. 1, p. 252.
135. Nicolay and Hay, ALCW, Vol. 2, p. 380. We will note here that there is a great difference between being an abolitionist and being antislavery. Authentic 19th-Century abolitionists (who were actually quite rare in the North) wanted enslaved blacks to be freed then given the exact same rights as whites. Antislavery advocates merely had a distaste for slavery, typically, as in Lincoln's case, because it forced whites to intermingle with blacks. Hence, Lincoln was indeed against slavery; but primarily only because it prevented he and other white separatists from being able to legally deport African-Americans "back to their native land," as he put it. See Nicolay and Hay, ALCW, Vol. 1, pp. 187, 288.
136. Nicolay and Hay, ALCW, Vol. 1, p. 252.
137. Nicolay and Hay, ALCW, Vol. 1, p. 252.
138. Nicolay and Hay, ALCW, Vol. 1, p. 569. See also p. 675.
139. Nicolay and Hay, ALCW, Vol. 1, p. 15. See also p. 642.
140. Nicolay and Hay, ALCW, Vol. 2, p. 1.
141. Current, LNK, pp. 218-219; W. B. Garrison, LNOK, pp. 35-37; Greenberg and Waugh, p. 355.
142. It has now been firmly established that the "Great Emancipator" used black slaves to build the White House, the U.S. Capitol, and numerous other Federal buildings in the city, along with many of her city streets. See De Angelis, pp. 12-18; Lott, p. 65; J. J. Holland, passim.
143. J. C. Perry, p. 191.
144. The National Almanac (1863), p. 250. See also Nicolay and Hay, ALCW, Vol. 2, pp. 144-145.
145. Nicolay and Hay, ALCW, Vol. 1, p. 306.
146. Nicolay and Hay, ALCW, Vol. 1, p. 659.
147. Berret later refused to take Lincoln's needless, spiteful, absurd, and illegal anti-South "Oath of Allegiance" to the United States, for which Lincoln had him arrested for "sedition" and sent to a military prison (illegal because Berret was a private citizen). This is just one example of how Lincoln treated those who supported him: Berret had loyally served on Lincoln's inaugural committee.
148. Nicolay and Hay, ALCW, Vol. 1, p. 694.
149. Cornish, p. 73; D. Brown, pp. 179-180; ORA, Ser. 3, Vol. 1, p. 184.
150. Buckley, p. 65. See also Greenberg and Waugh, pp. 351-358.
151. Shotwell, p. 436.
152. Nicolay and Hay, ALCW, Vol. 1, p. 288. See also p. 187.
153. Gilmore, p. 199.
154. Nicolay and Hay, ALCW, Vol. 2, p. 420.
155. Nicolay and Hay, ALCW, Vol. 1, p. 331.
156. Kennedy, p. 91.
157. Seabrook, TQJD, p. 68.
158. M. M. Smith, pp. 4-5. Lincoln once acknowledged this fact when he said: "In most of the southern states, a majority of the whole people of all colors are neither slaves nor masters . . ." Nicolay and Hay, ALCW, Vol. 1, p. 581.
159. To learn the truth about Alexander H. Stephens' remark about slavery being the "cornerstone" of the Confederacy, see Seabrook, TQAHS, and Seabrook, TAHSR.
160. For more on this topic see Seabrook, EYWTACWW, pp. 86-89.
161. Seabrook, EYWTAASIW, pp. 48, 549, 550.
162. See e.g., Jefferson's antislavery views in his rough draft of the Declaration of Independence, written in 1776. Foley, p. 970.
163. Seabrook, AL, pp. 187-239.
164. Seabrook, EYWTACWW, p. 95.

165. Seabrook, EYWTACWW, p. 81.
166. Seabrook, EYWTACWW, pp. 77-80.
167. Seabrook, EYWTACWW, p. 77.
168. Seabrook, TQJD, p. 67.
169. Seabrook, EYWTACWW, p. 95.
170. For the full true story of American slavery, see Seabrook, EYWTAASIW.
171. Foote, Vol. 1, p. 537.
172. Nicolay and Hay, ALCW, Vol. 2, pp. 121-122.
173. Farrow, Lang, and Frank, pp. 131-132.
174. Kennedy, pp. 104-105.
175. Nicolay and Hay, ALCW, Vol. 2, p. 101.
176. Nicolay and Hay, ALCW, Vol. 1, p. 197.
177. Nicolay and Hay, ALCW, Vol. 1, p. 559.
178. Nicolay and Hay, ALCW, Vol. 1, p. 569.
179. Nicolay and Hay, ALCW, Vol. 1, p. 253.
180. Nicolay and Hay, ALCW, Vol. 1, p. 534.
181. See Findlay and Findlay, p. 164.
182. Nicolay and Hay, ALCW, Vol. 1, pp. 306-307.
183. Nicolay and Hay, ALCW, Vol. 1, p. 307.
184. Nicolay and Hay, ALCW, Vol. 1, pp. 657-658.
185. Nicolay and Hay, ALCW, Vol. 1, p. 669.
186. Nicolay and Hay, ALCW, Vol. 1, p. 307.
187. Nicolay and Hay, ALCW, Vol. 1, p. 307.
188. Nicolay and Hay, ALCW, Vol. 1, p. 308.
189. Nicolay and Hay, ALCW, Vol. 1, p. 187.
190. Nicolay and Hay, CWAL, Vol. 1, pp. 275-277.
191. Nicolay and Hay, ALCW, Vol. 1, p. 199.
192. Nicolay and Hay, ALCW, Vol. 1, p. 273. In light of the fact that 95.2 percent of Southerners did not own slaves (in 1860), and that nearly all these were abolitionists, Lincoln's fear of a Southern right-wing conspiracy to nationalize slavery is completely absurd. Still, even though he knew it was a lie, he continued to try and whip up anti-South sentiment in the North with such false and misleading statements as: "I clearly see, as I think, a powerful plot to make slavery universal and perpetual in this nation." Nicolay and Hay, ALCW, Vol. 1, p. 418.
193. Nicolay and Hay, ALCW, Vol. 1, p. 347.
194. Nicolay and Hay, ALCW, Vol. 1, p. 369.
195. Nicolay and Hay, ALCW, Vol. 1, p. 652.
196. Nicolay and Hay, ALCW, Vol. 1, p. 408.
197. Nicolay and Hay, ALCW, Vol. 1, p. 658. We will note here that, as he usually was about such matters, Lincoln was wrong, making assumptions about the South that were quite false: Gilmer, along with most other Southerners did not want to extend slavery. They merely wanted the states and the Western Territories to have the choice of whether to accept or reject slavery. Being a Liberal, Lincoln wanted his view imposed on the entire nation, even if it was against the will of the majority of people.
198. Nicolay and Hay, ALCW, Vol. 2, p. 268.
199. Nicolay and Hay, ALCW, Vol. 1, p. 556.
200. Nicolay and Hay, ALCW, Vol. 1, p. 197.
201. Nicolay and Hay, ALCW, Vol. 1, p. 196.
202. Nicolay and Hay, ALCW, Vol. 1, p. 193.
203. Nicolay and Hay, ALCW, Vol. 1, p. 463.
204. Current, LNK, p. 225.
205. W. B. Garrison, LNOK, p. 181.
206. Nicolay and Hay, ALCW, Vol. 2, p. 550.
207. Nicolay and Hay, ALCW, Vol. 1, p. 288. See also p. 187.
208. Current, LNK, p. 245.
209. Litwack, NS, p. 277.
210. Nicolay and Hay, ALCW, Vol. 2, p. 296; Current, LNK, pp. 239-240.
211. Nicolay and Hay, ALAH, Vol. 10, p. 123; DiLorenzo, LU, pp. 24, 25.
212. L. Johnson, p. 141.
213. W. S. Powell, p. 144.
214. See Current, LNK, pp. 223, 239, 240, 241.
215. Nicolay and Hay, ALCW, Vol. 2, p. 529.
216. Nicolay and Hay, ALCW, Vol. 2, pp. 563-564.
217. Nicolay and Hay, ALCW, Vol. 1, p. 508.
218. Rutherford, FA, p. 38; Wallechinsky, Wallace, and Wallace, p. 11; Woods, p. 67.
219. McElroy, p. 357.
220. *Appendix to the Congressional Globe*, 29th Congress, 2nd Session, February 8, 1847, p. 317.
221. Nicolay and Hay, ALCW, Vol. 1, p. 273.

222. Catton, Vol. 1, p. 86.
223. Nicolay and Hay, ALCW, Vol. 1, pp. 668-669.
224. Nicolay and Hay, ALCW, Vol. 1, pp. 585-586.
225. Rosenbaum and Brinkley, s.v. "Wilmot Proviso."
226. Weintraub, p. 64.
227. *Appendix to the Congressional Globe*, 29th Congress, 2nd Session, February 8, 1847, p. 317.
228. Nicolay and Hay, ALCW, Vol. 1, p. 218. See also p. 184.
229. Nicolay and Hay, ALCW, Vol. 1, p. 199.
230. Nicolay and Hay, ALCW, Vol. 1, p. 605.
231. C. Adams, p. 159.
232. Nicolay and Hay, ALCW, Vol. 1, p. 608. Jefferson's words are from his autobiography, written in 1821, when he was seventy-seven years old. See Foley, p. 816.
233. Nicolay and Hay, ALCW, Vol. 1, p. 612.
234. Nicolay and Hay, ALCW, Vol. 1, pp. 657-658.
235. Seabrook, EYWTAASIW, pp. 62-229.
236. Nicolay and Hay, ALCW, Vol. 1, p. 197.
237. Nicolay and Hay, ALCW, Vol. 1, p. 418.
238. M. Davis, p. 49.
239. DiLorenzo, LU, p. 24.
240. Beard and Beard, Vol. 2, p. 65.
241. Nicolay and Hay, ALCW, Vol. 2, p. 296.
242. Nicolay and Hay, ALAH, Vol. 10, p. 123. See also DiLorenzo, LU, p. 25.
243. Nicolay and Hay, ALCW, Vol. 2, p. 6.
244. Lamon, RAL, p. 173.
245. Christian, p. 27.
246. Seabrook, AL, pp. 295-321.
247. Seabrook, EYWTACWW, pp. 35-39.
248. See Napolitano, p. 8.
249. Thornton and Ekelund, pp. 98-99.
250. C. Adams, pp. 198-199; Woods, p. 75; Website: www.lewrockwell.com/org/mencken2.html.
251. A. Cooke, ACA, p. 214.
252. For more on the widespread destruction Lincoln intentionally inflicted on the South, see Seabrook, TUC.
253. Nicolay and Hay, ALCW, Vol. 1, pp. 186-187. See also p. 288.
254. Nicolay and Hay, ALCW, Vol. 1, p. 194.
255. That is, the good side of his nature, as opposed to the evil one. See Nicolay and Hay, ALCW, Vol. 2, p. 7.
256. J. M. McPherson, ACW, p. 9. See also Seabrook, TUC, passim.
257. Fehrenbacher and Fehrenbacher, p. 539. Pierce mentions this conversation (though not Lincoln's use of the "n" word) in an *Atlantic Monthly* article entitled "The Freedman of Port Royal," Volume 12, September 1863, pp. 296-297. Lincoln refers to Pierce in a letter to Salmon P. Chase on February 15, 1862. See Basler, CWAL, p. 132.
258. See e.g., Nicolay and Hay, ALCW, Vol. 1, p. 524; Neely, p. 213.
259. See e.g., Nicolay and Hay, ALCW, Vol. 1, p. 449.
260. See e.g., Nicolay and Hay, ALCW, Vol. 1, p. 449.
261. Nicolay and Hay, ALCW, Vol. 1, p. 7.
262. U.S. gov. Website: www.nps.gov/gett/forteachers/upload/7%20Lincoln%20on%20Race.pdf.
263. Nicolay and Hay, ALCW, Vol. 1, p. 292.
264. Bryan, p. 291.
265. Nicolay and Hay, ALCW, Vol. 1, p. 298.
266. Lincoln and Douglas, p. 95.
267. Nicolay and Hay, ALCW, Vol. 1, p. 556.
268. Nicolay and Hay, ALCW, Vol. 1, p. 257.
269. Nicolay and Hay, ALCW, Vol. 1, p. 208.
270. Arnett, p. 758.
271. Nicolay and Hay, CWAL, Vol. 11, pp. 105-106.
272. Nicolay and Hay, ALCW, Vol. 1, p. 369. See also p. 539.
273. Nicolay and Hay, ALCW, Vol. 1, pp. 369-370.
274. Nicolay and Hay, ALCW, Vol. 1, p. 370.
275. Nicolay and Hay, ALCW, Vol. 1, p. 370.
276. Nicolay and Hay, ALCW, Vol. 1, p. 370.
277. Nicolay and Hay, ALCW, Vol. 5, pp. 87, 89.
278. Nicolay and Hay, ALCW, Vol. 1, p. 556.
279. Nicolay and Hay, ALCW, Vol. 1, p. 563.
280. Nicolay and Hay, ALCW, Vol. 1, p. 614.
281. Nicolay and Hay, ALCW, Vol. 1, p. 569.

282. Nicolay and Hay, ALCW, Vol. 1, p. 355.
283. America's history of black racism and black racial separatism is nearly as long as that of whites. See e.g., Blassingame, p. 25; Garraty and McCaughey, p. 145; Adams and Sanders, p. 228; Rosenbaum, s.v. "Garvey, Marcus Moziah"; Rosenbaum, s.v. "Delaney, Martin Robinson"; Rosenbaum and Brinkley, s.v. "Back to Africa"; "Colonization." Like Lincoln and most other 19th-Century white Northerners, the majority of today's black racists are against interracial marriage and for racial separation.
284. As we have seen, Lincoln publicly agreed with Senator Stephen A. Douglas' comment that "the inferior race [blacks] bears the superior [whites] down." See Nicolay and Hay, ALCW, Vol. 1, p. 257.
285. On numerous occasions Lincoln stated that he would never marry a black woman. See e.g., Nicolay and Hay, ALCW, Vol. 1, p. 569.
286. Nicolay and Hay, ALCW, Vol. 1, pp. 231-232.
287. Lincoln was referring to "nearly all *Northern* white people." He repeatedly demonstrated that he knew almost nothing about how Southern whites felt toward blacks.
288. See Seabrook, EYWTACWW, passim.
289. "A very fair proportion of the people of Louisiana," Lincoln stated on November 14, 1864, "have inaugurated a new state government, making an excellent new constitution—better for the poor black man than we have in Illinois." Nicolay and Hay, ALCW, Vol. 2, p. 597.
290. Lincoln himself was often referred to, not as a Southerner or a Northerner, but as a "Westerner."
291. Nicolay and Hay, ALCW, Vol. 1, p. 196.
292. Basler, ALSW, pp. 382-383.
293. Rosenbaum, s.v. "Mexican War." See also Buckley, p. 67.
294. DeGregorio, s.v. "James K. Polk."
295. Nicolay and Hay, ALCW, Vol. 1, p. 134. This paragraph is from what Nicolay and Hay called a "fragment" of a paper written by Lincoln "as being what he thought General [Zachary] Taylor ought to say." The statement was for Taylor, but it reflected Lincoln's thinking. Whig Lincoln was a supporter of Taylor, the Whigs' presidential candidate, for the upcoming election on November 7, 1848. Taylor won over Democrat (then the Conservative party) Lewis Cass and Free Soiler Martin Van Buren with nearly 50 percent of the American vote, becoming our twelfth president.
296. Nicolay and Hay, ALCW, Vol. 1, pp. 234-235.
297. Nicolay and Hay, ALCW, Vol. 1, p. 235.
298. Fogel, pp. 386-387.
299. Nicolay and Hay, ALCW, Vol. 1, pp. 370, 539.
300. Nicolay and Hay, ALCW, Vol. 5, p. 89.
301. See e.g., Nicolay and Hay, ALCW, Vol. 1, p. 449.
302. Nicolay and Hay, ALCW, Vol. 1, p. 449.
303. Seabrook, EYWTACWW, pp. 63-70.
304. Seabrook, AL, pp. 257-258.
305. Nicolay and Hay, ALCW, Vol. 1, pp. 406-407.
306. Nicolay and Hay, ALCW, Vol. 1, p. 272.
307. Nicolay and Hay, ALCW, Vol. 1, p. 539. See also pp. 369, 432, 457, 470.
308. Nicolay and Hay, ALCW, Vol. 1, p. 187.
309. Nicolay and Hay, ALCW, Vol. 1, p. 438.
310. See Litwack, passim.
311. Nicolay and Hay, CWAL, Vol. 3, p. 354.
312. Nicolay and Hay, ALCW, Vol. 1, p. 540.
313. Nicolay and Hay, ALCW, Vol. 2, p. 674.
314. Foner, R, p. 74.
315. See Seabrook, EYWTACWW, pp. 167-176.
316. Nicolay and Hay, ALCW, Vol. 1, p. 502.
317. Fogel, p. 252.
318. Website: www.slavenorth.com/colonize.htm.
319. Nye, p. 20.
320. Meltzer, Vol. 2, p. 139; Cartmell, p. 26; Norwood, p. 31.
321. G. H. Moore, pp. 5, 11, 17-19.
322. Some 12,000 to 15,000 American blacks were eventually deported to Liberia, many of them under Lincoln. But their "liberation" was short-lived: conditions were so despicable that hundreds died before they could find a way back to the U.S. To this day, the descendants of these 19th-Century inhabitants are still called "Americo-Liberians," and make up 10 percent of the nation's population. This group is to be contrasted with the other 90 percent, the native, indigenous population of Africans, with whom they share ongoing rivalries and disputes in this, Africa's oldest black republic. Rosenbaum, s.v. "Liberia"; Nye, p. 17; Brunner, s.v. "Liberia."
323. Nicolay and Hay, ALCW, Vol. 1, p. 175.
324. W. B. Garrison, LNOK, p. 186; DiLorenzo, LU, p. 28.
325. Nicolay and Hay, ALCW, Vol. 1, p. 299.
326. W. B. Garrison, LNOK, p. 186; DiLorenzo, LU, p. 28.
327. Nicolay and Hay, ALCW, Vol. 1, p. 448.
328. Nicolay and Hay, ALCW, Vol. 1, p. 273.
329. For more on Lincoln's socialistic tendencies, see Seabrook, AL, pp. 488-493.
330. Nicolay and Hay, ALCW, Vol. 1, p. 564.
331. Nicolay and Hay, ALCW, Vol. 1, p. 613.

332. See Nicolay and Hay, ALCW, Vol. 1, p. 175.
333. Nicolay and Hay, ALCW, Vol. 1, p. 299.
334. Nicolay and Hay, ALCW, Vol. 1, p. 174.
335. Nicolay and Hay, ALCW, Vol. 1, pp. 175-176.
336. Nicolay and Hay, ALAH, Vol. 6, p. 356. See also pp. 357-358.
337. Nicolay and Hay, ALCW, Vol. 2, pp. 102-103.
338. De Angelis, p. 49.
339. W. Wilson, DR, p. 125.
340. Nicolay and Hay, ALCW, Vol. 2, pp. 144-145.
341. *The National Almanac* (1863), p. 250.
342. Nicolay and Hay, ALCW, Vol. 2, p. 144.
343. Nicolay and Hay, ALCW, Vol. 2, p. 205.
344. Nicolay and Hay, ALCW, Vol. 1, pp. 187, 288.
345. Nicolay and Hay, ALCW, Vol. 1, p. 174.
346. Nicolay and Hay, ALCW, Vol. 2, pp. 262-263.
347. See Bennett, passim. See also DiLorenzo, LU, pp. 28, 49.
348. Cornish, p. 95.
349. Nicolay and Hay, ALCW, Vol. 2, p. 270.
350. Nicolay and Hay, ALCW, Vol. 2, p. 271.
351. Nicolay and Hay, ALCW, Vol. 2, p. 271.
352. Nicolay and Hay, ALCW, Vol. 2, p. 274.
353. Nicolay and Hay, ALCW, Vol. 2, p. 274.
354. Nicolay and Hay, ALCW, Vol. 1, p. 271.
355. C. Johnson, p. 182.
356. Lemire, passim.
357. Nicolay and Hay, ALCW, Vol. 2, p. 477.
358. Nicolay and Hay, ALCW, Vol. 2, p. 605.
359. W. P. Pickett, p. 317.
360. C. Johnson, p. 182.
361. Seabrook, EYWTACWW, pp. 147-148.
362. Nicolay and Hay, ALCW, Vol. 2, pp. 237-238.
363. Nicolay and Hay, ALCW, Vol. 2, pp. 222-225.
364. R. L. Riley, p. 109.
365. Oates, AL, p. 103. See also Janessa Hoyte, "Taking Another Look at Abraham Lincoln," *The Crisis*, November/December 2000, pp. 52-54.
366. *Douglass' Monthly*, September 1862, Vol. 5, pp. 707-708.
367. Nicolay and Hay, ALCW, Vol. 2, p. 495.
368. Seabrook, AL, pp. 417, 520.
369. B. F. Butler, p. 903. See also W. P. Pickett, p. 326; M. Davis, pp. 147-148; Adams and Sanders, p. 192.
370. B. F. Butler, p. 903. See also W. P. Pickett, pp. 326-327.
371. B. F. Butler, p. 907.
372. W. Phillips, p. 456.
373. Meriwether, p. 9.
374. Nicolay and Hay, ALCW, Vol. 2, p. 234.
375. Nicolay and Hay, ALCW, Vol. 2, pp. 287-288.
376. D. H. Donald, LR, p. 203.
377. Nicolay and Hay, ALCW, Vol. 2, pp. 402-403.
378. Nicolay and Hay, ALCW, Vol. 2, p. 234.
379. Nicolay and Hay, ALCW, Vol. 2, p. 453.
380. For more on the many reasons Lincoln actually issued the Emancipation Proclamation, see Seabrook, L, pp. 634-697.
381. Coffin, pp. 330-331; Nicolay and Hay, ALCW, Vol. 2, p. 479.
382. Nicolay and Hay, ALCW, Vol. 2, pp. 508-509.
383. Nicolay and Hay, ALCW, Vol. 2, p. 235.
384. Nicolay and Hay, ALCW, Vol. 2, p. 397.
385. Rosenbaum and Brinkley, s.v. "Lincoln and Douglas."
386. Thornton and Ekelund, p. 96.
387. Haggard, p. 90.
388. Stephens, RAHS, pp. 83, 137; Stephens, CV, Vol. 2, p. 615.
389. See e.g., Nicolay and Hay, ALCW, Vol. 2, pp. 192-193.
390. Seabrook, EYWTACWW, pp. 157-166.
391. Seabrook, EYWTACWW, p. 167.
392. Nicolay and Hay, ALCW, Vol. 2, p. 562.
393. W. B. Garrison, LNOK, pp. 174-177.

394. L. Johnson, p. 133.
395. Mullen, p. 22.
396. Nicolay and Hay, ALCW, Vol. 2, p. 576.
397. As we have seen, on August 17, 1864, Lincoln said: "When I afterward proclaimed emancipation, and employed colored soldiers [in the army] . . ." Nicolay and Hay, ALCW, Vol. 2, p. 564.
398. Nicolay and Hay, ALCW, Vol. 2, p. 288.
399. Nicolay and Hay, ALCW, Vol. 2, p. 398.
400. Nicolay and Hay, ALCW, Vol. 2, p. 288.
401. Nicolay and Hay, ALCW, Vol. 2, p. 384.
402. Nicolay and Hay, ALCW, Vol. 2, p. 298.
403. ORA, Ser. 3, Vol. 2, p. 314.
404. Nicolay and Hay, ALCW, Vol. 2, p. 318.
405. Lincoln was completely wrong in this assumption. See Seabrook, EYWTACWW, pp. 188-192.
406. Nicolay and Hay, ALCW, Vol. 2, p. 235. Lincoln had a right to be worried. In thousands of cases this is precisely what happened.
407. Nicolay and Hay, ALCW, Vol. 2, pp. 215-216.
408. For more on these relationships, see Seabrook, LW; Seabrook, ALWALJDWAC.
409. Nicolay and Hay, ALAH, Vol. 9, p. 184.
410. For Greeley's complete letter see Brockett, pp. 308-315. We will note here that *everything* Greeley says in his letter to Lincoln concerning the South is false. Since it is outside the scope of this book to address all of these falsehoods and slanders, I direct the reader to my books that do: *Lincoln's War: The Real Cause, the Real Winner, the Real Loser*; *All We Ask is to be Let Alone: The Southern Secession Fact Book*; *Rise Up and Call Them Blessed: Victorian Tributes to the Confederate Soldier, 1861-1901*; *Everything You Were Taught About the Civil War Is Wrong, Ask A Southerner!*; *Everything You Were Taught About American Slavery Is Wrong, Ask A Southerner!*; *A Rebel Born: A Defense of Nathan Bedford Forrest*; *Abraham Lincoln: The Southern View*; *The Quotable Jefferson Davis*; *The Quotable Alexander H. Stephens*, etc.
411. Nicolay and Hay, ALCW, Vol. 2, pp. 227-228.
412. Note: the "public safety" was not in danger due to the pro-Confederate movement in Kentucky, and those who supported it were not in "rebellion" against the United States. Therefore Lincoln's suspension of *habeas corpus* in the Bluegrass State was both illegal and unnecessary. The real purpose behind these crimes was Liberal Lincoln's autocratic desire to silence those who disagreed with him.
413. Nicolay and Hay, ALCW, Vol. 2, pp. 541-543.
414. L. Johnson, p. 124.
415. Grissom, p. 155; Rutland, p. 226; Neely, pp. 113-116; Dilorenzo, LU, p. 168.
416. Nicolay and Hay, ALCW, Vol. 2, p. 70.
417. Nicolay and Hay, ALCW, Vol. 2, p. 79.
418. Nicolay and Hay, ALCW, Vol. 2, p. 59.
419. Seabrook, L, pp. 750-751; Seabrook, AWAITBLA, p. 200.
420. See Findlay and Findlay, pp. 196-197.
421. Nicolay and Hay, ALCW, Vol. 2, pp. 523-524.
422. Nicolay and Hay, ALCW, Vol. 2, p. 349.
423. Findlay and Findlay, pp. 168-169.
424. Seabrook, AWAITBLA, p. 200.
425. L. Johnson, p. 125. See also e.g., Nicolay and Hay, ALCW, Vol. 2, p. 416.
426. Burns and Peltason, p. 192. For other examples of Lincoln's suspension of *habeas corpus*, see Nicolay and Hay, ALCW, Vol. 2, pp. 39, 54, 85, 93, 239, 406-407. See also Nicolay and Hay, ALCW, Vol. 2, pp. 541-542.
427. Neely, pp. 172-175.
428. C. Adams, p. 210; W. B. Garrison, CWTFB, p. 62; D. H. Donald, L, 392-395.
429. Tatalovich and Daynes, p. 322.
430. See e.g., Nicolay and Hay, ALCW, Vol. 2, pp. 486, 489-490.
431. Mitgang, p. 402; D. H. Donald, L, p. 385.
432. W. B. Garrison, CWC, p. 13; Findlay and Findlay, pp. 84-85; C. Adams, p. 39; Owsley, pp. 79-80, 229-267; K. L. Hall, s.v. "Lincoln, Abraham"; "Civil War."
433. Nicolay and Hay, ALCW, Vol. 2, pp. 464, 491.
434. J. Davis, RFCG, Vol. 2, pp. 460-468.
435. Tatalovich and Daynes, p. 322.
436. W. B. Garrison, LNOK, p. 281.
437. Burns and Peltason, p. 437.
438. "Freedom Watch," FOX Business News, March 24, 2010.
439. J. Davis, RFCG, Vol. 2, pp. 460-468. For more on Lincoln's illegal subjugation of Maryland, see Pollard, LC, pp. 123-125.
440. Hacker, p. 584; Napolitano, p. 74.
441. Christian, p. 14; Hacker, p. 581.
442. Lincoln knew this was unconstitutional, which is why he brought the issue up with his cabinet members on December 23, 1862. Nicolay and Hay, ALCW, Vol. 2, p. 283. Note: It is illegal for a section of a state to secede from the parent state without the parent's state's approval. Virginia never authorized the secession of West Virginia. C. Adams, p. 58. See also W. B. Garrison, LNOK, pp. 193-197; D. H. Donald, L, pp. 300-301, 405; DiLorenzo, RL, pp. 148-149.
443. L. Johnson, pp. 123-124; Horn, IE, p. 217; DiLorenzo, LU, p. 52; Simpson, p. 62.

444. W. B. Garrison, ACW, pp. 194-195; DeGregorio, s.v. "Abraham Lincoln"; D. H. Donald, L, p. 249.
445. Wiley, SN, pp. 241, 309-310, 317; L. Johnson, p. 134.
446. See e.g., Nicolay and Hay, ALCW, Vol. 2, p. 521. Lincoln's preferred methods of torture were "violent cold water torture" and being suspended by handcuffed wrists. Neely, pp. 109-112.
447. Nicolay and Hay, ALCW, Vol. 2, p. 216.
448. See Seabrook, AWAITBLA, passim.
449. Seabrook, AL, pp. 81-102.
450. Nicolay and Hay, ALCW, Vol. 2, p. 620.
451. In his Final Emancipation Proclamation Lincoln clearly states that he issued the edict, not for black civil rights, but as a "war measure," one based on "military necessity." These two phrases were nothing more than a euphemism for "needing more soldiers and more votes." As such, the Emancipation Proclamation is glaring in its total lack of any reference to black civil rights. See Nicolay and Hay, ALCW, Vol. 2, pp. 287-288.
452. Nicolay and Hay, ALCW, Vol. 2, p. 216.
453. Nicolay and Hay, ALCW, Vol. 2, p. 81.
454. Nicolay and Hay, ALCW, Vol. 2, p. 621.
455. Nicolay and Hay, ALCW, Vol. 2, pp. 629-630.
456. Seabrook, L, p. 823.
457. Nicolay and Hay, ALCW, Vol. 2, p. 561.
458. Nicolay and Hay, ALCW, Vol. 2, p. 508.
459. Oates, AL, pp. 5, 40; Current, LNK, p. 60.
460. Mary, despondent over her young son Willie's death (on February 20, 1862), held at least eight known seances at the White House in an attempt to contact her boy on the Other Side. Her atheist husband, however, would have none of it: Mr. Lincoln pronounced all of Mary's spiritualist efforts horse feathers and flapdoodle—this despite the fact that, according to Mary herself, Willie punctually appeared to her at the foot of her bed night after night. D. H. Donald, L, p. 427.
461. Kane, p. 163.
462. *Southern Review*, January 1873, Vol. 12, No. 25, p. 364.
463. Current, LNK, pp. 58, 61.
464. Oates, AL, p. 53.
465. Current, LNK, p. 58.
466. Lamon, LAL, p. 488.
467. W. B. Garrison, LNOK, p. 265.
468. Christian, p. 7.
469. Ashe, p. 62.
470. Minor, p. 25.
471. Nicolay and Hay, ALCW, Vol. 1, p. 16.
472. J. G. Holland, p. 236.
473. Remsburg, p. 292.
474. Remsburg, p. 292.
475. Remsburg, p. 296.
476. Minor, p. 49; DeGregorio, s.v. "Abraham Lincoln"; Beschloss, p. 113; K. C. Davis, p. 219; Flood, p. 37; D. H. Donald, L, p. 319.
477. The pseudonym of Charles Farrar Browne, a popular 19th-Century humorist and writer from Maine.
478. For more on this obscene incident, see Seabrook, AL, pp. 470-471.
479. Rice, RAL, p. 352.
480. *The Congressional Globe*, 37th Congress, 3rd Session, pp. 549, 550.
481. Julian, pp. 241-242.
482. Lamon, LAL, p. 489.
483. Christian, pp. 15, 17, 20.
484. Meriwether, p. 13.
485. Seabrook, AL, p. 262.
486. *House Documents*, p. 92.
487. Shotwell, p. 436.

BIBLIOGRAPHY

Adams, Charles. *When in the Course of Human Events: Arguing the Case for Southern Secession.* Lanham, MD: Rowman and Littlefield, 2000.
Adams, Francis D., and Barry Sanders. *Alienable Rights: The Exclusion of African Americans in a White Man's Land, 1619-2000.* 2003. New York, NY: Perennial, 2004 ed.
Arnett, Benjamin William (ed.). *Duplicate Copy of the Souvenir From the Afro-American League of Tennessee to Honorable James M. Ashley of Ohio.* Philadelphia, PA: A. M. E. Church, 1894.
Ashe, Captain Samuel A'Court. *A Southern View of the Invasion of the Southern States and War of 1861-1865.* 1935. Crawfordville, GA: Ruffin Flag Co., 1938 ed.
Basler, Roy Prentice (ed.). *Abraham Lincoln: His Speeches and Writings.* 1946. New York, NY: Da Capo Press, 2001 ed.
——— (ed.). *The Collected Works of Abraham Lincoln.* 9 vols. New Brunswick, NJ: Rutgers University Press, 1953.
Beard, Charles A., and Mary R. Beard. *The Rise of American Civilization.* 1927. New York, NY: MacMillan, 1930 ed.
Bennett, Lerone. *Forced into Glory: Abraham Lincoln's White Dream.* Chicago, IL: Johnson Publishing Co., 2000.
Beschloss, Michael R. *Presidential Courage: Brave Leaders and How They Changed America, 1789-1989.* New York, NY: Simon and Schuster, 2007.
Black, Robert W., Col. *Cavalry Raids of the Civil War.* Mechanicsburg, PA: Stackpole, 2004.
Blassingame, John W. *The Slave Community: Plantation Life in the Antebellum South.* 1972. New York, NY: Oxford University Press, 1974 ed.
Brockett, Linus Pierpont. *The Life and Times of Abraham Lincoln, Sixteenth President of the United States.* Philadelphia, PA: Bradley and Co., 1865.
Brown, Dee. *Bury My Heart at Wounded Knee: An Indian History of the American West.* 1970. New York, NY: Owl Books, 1991 ed.
Brunner, Borgna (ed.). *The Time Almanac (1999 ed.).* Boston, MA: Information Please, 1998.
Bryan, William Jennings. *The Commoner Condensed.* New York, NY: Abbey Press, 1902.
Buckley, Gail. *American Patriots: The Story of Blacks in the Military From the Revolution to Desert Storm.* New York, NY: Random House, 2001.
Burns, James MacGregor, and Jack Walter Peltason. *Government by the People: The Dynamics of American National, State, and Local Government.* 1952. Englewood Cliffs, NJ: Prentice-Hall, 1964 ed.
Butler, Benjamin Franklin. *Butler's Book (Autobiography and Personal Reminiscences of Major-General Benjamin F. Butler: A Review of His Legal, Political, and Military Career).* Boston, MA: A. M. Thayer and Co., 1892.
Cartmell, Donald. *Civil War 101.* New York, NY: Gramercy, 2001.
Catton, Bruce. *The Coming Fury (Vol. 1).* 1961. New York, NY: Washington Square Press, 1967 ed.
Christian, George L. *Abraham Lincoln: An Address Delivered Before R. E. Lee Camp, No. 1 Confederate Veterans at Richmond, VA, October 29, 1909.* Richmond, VA: L. H. Jenkins, 1909.
Coffin, Charles Carleton. *Abraham Lincoln.* New York, NY: Harper and Brothers, 1893.
Cooke, Alistair. *Alistair Cooke's America.* 1973. New York, NY: Alfred A. Knopf, 1984 ed.
Cornish, Dudley Taylor. *The Sable Arm: Black Troops in the Union Army, 1861-1865.* 1956. Lawrence, KS: University Press of Kansas, 1987 ed.
Current, Richard N. *The Lincoln Nobody Knows.* 1958. New York, NY: Hill and Wang, 1963 ed.
Davis, Jefferson. *The Rise and Fall of the Confederate Government.* 2 vols. New York, NY: D. Appleton and Co., 1881.
———. *A Short History of the Confederate States of America.* New York, NY: Belford, 1890.
Davis, Kenneth C. *Don't Know Much About the Civil War: Everything You Need to Know About America's Greatest Conflict But Never Learned.* 1996. New York, NY: HarperCollins, 1997 ed.
Davis, Michael. *The Image of Lincoln in the South.* Knoxville, TN: University of Tennessee Press, 1971.
De Angelis, Gina. *It Happened in Washington, D.C.* Guilford, CT: Globe Pequot Press, 2004.
DeGregorio, William A. *The Complete Book of U.S. Presidents.* 1984. New York, NY: Barricade, 1993 ed.
DiLorenzo, Thomas J. "The Great Centralizer: Abraham Lincoln and the War Between the States." *The Independent Review*, Vol. 3, No. 2, Fall 1998, pp. 243-271.
———. *The Real Lincoln: A New Look at Abraham Lincoln, His Agenda, and an Unnecessary War.* Three Rivers, MI: Three Rivers Press, 2003.
———. *Lincoln Unmasked: What You're Not Supposed to Know About Dishonest Abe.* New York, NY: Crown Forum, 2006.
Donald, David Herbert. *Lincoln Reconsidered: Essays on the Civil War Era.* 1947. New York, NY: Vintage Press, 1989 ed.
——— (ed.). *Why the North Won the Civil War.* 1960. New York, NY: Collier, 1962 ed.
———. *Lincoln.* New York, NY: Simon and Schuster, 1995.
Farrow, Anne, Joel Lang, and Jennifer Frank. *Complicity: How the North Promoted, Prolonged, and Profited From Slavery.* New York, NY: Ballantine, 2005.
Fehrenbacher, Don E., and Virginia Fehrenbacher (eds). *Recollected Works of Abraham Lincoln.* Stanford, CA: Stanford University Press, 1996.
Findlay, Bruce, and Esther Findlay. *Your Rugged Constitution: How America's House of Freedom is Planned and Built.* 1950. Stanford, CA: Stanford University Press, 1951 ed.
Flood, Charles Bracelen. *1864: Lincoln At the Gates of History.* New York, NY: Simon and Schuster, 2009.
Fogel, Robert William. *Without Consent or Contract: The Rise and Fall of American Slavery.* New York, NY: W. W. Norton, 1989.
Foley, John P. (ed.). *The Jeffersonian Cyclopedia.* New York, NY: Funk and Wagnalls, 1900.
Foner, Eric. *Reconstruction: America's Unfinished Revolution, 1863-1877.* 1988. New York, NY: Harper and Row, 1989 ed.
Foote, Shelby. *The Civil War: A Narrative, Fort Sumter to Perryville, Vol. 1.* 1958. New York, NY: Vintage, 1986 ed.
———. *The Civil War: A Narrative, Fredericksburg to Meridian, Vol. 2.* 1963. New York, NY: Vintage, 1986 ed.

——. *The Civil War: A Narrative, Red River to Appomattox, Vol. 3.* 1974. New York, NY: Vintage, 1986 ed.
Garraty, John A., and Robert A. McCaughey. *A Short History of the American Nation.* 1966. New York, NY: HarperCollins, 1989 ed.
Garrison, Webb B. *Civil War Trivia and Fact Book.* Nashville, TN: Rutledge Hill Press, 1992.
——. *The Lincoln No One Knows: The Mysterious Man Who Ran the Civil War.* Nashville, TN: Rutledge Hill Press, 1993.
——. *Civil War Curiosities: Strange Stories, Oddities, Events, and Coincidences.* Nashville, TN: Rutledge Hill Press, 1994.
——. *The Amazing Civil War.* Nashville, TN: Rutledge Hill Press, 1998.
Gilmore, James Roberts. *Personal Recollections of Abraham Lincoln and the Civil War.* Boston, MA: L. C. Page and Co., 1898.
Gordon, Armistead Churchill. *Figures From American History: Jefferson Davis.* New York, NY: Charles Scribner's Sons, 1918.
Greenberg, Martin H., and Charles G. Waugh (eds.). *The Price of Freedom: Slavery and the Civil War—Vol. 1, The Demise of Slavery.* Nashville, TN: Cumberland House, 2000.
Grissom, Michael Andrew. *Southern By the Grace of God.* 1988. Gretna, LA: Pelican Publishing Co., 1995 ed.
Hacker, Louis Morton. *The Shaping of the American Tradition.* New York, NY: Columbia University Press, 1947.
Haggard, Dixie Ray (ed.). *African Americans in the Nineteenth Century: People and Perspectives.* Santa Barbara, CA: ABC-Clio, 2010.
Hall, Kermit L. (ed). *The Oxford Companion to the Supreme Court of the United States.* New York, NY: Oxford University Press, 1992.
Hayden, Horace Edwin. *Virginia Genealogies: A Genealogy of the Glassell Family of Scotland and Virginia.* 1885. Wilkes-Barre, PA: N.P., 1891 ed.
Holland, Jesse J. *Black Men Built the Capitol: Discovering African-American History in and Around Washington, D.C.* Guilford, CT: The Globe Pequot Press, 2007.
Holland, Josiah Gilbert. *The Life of Abraham Lincoln.* Springfield, MA: Gurdon Bill, 1866.
Horn, Stanley F. *Invisible Empire: The Story of the Ku Klux Klan, 1866-1871.* 1939. Montclair, NJ: Patterson Smith, 1969 ed.
House Documents, 64th Congress, 1st Session, December 6, 1915, to September 8, 1916, Vol. 145. Washington, D.C.: Government Printing Office, 1916.
Johnson, Clint. *The Politically Incorrect Guide to the South (and Why It Will Rise Again).* Washington, D.C.: Regnery, 2006.
Johnson, Ludwell H. *North Against South: The American Iliad, 1848-1877.* 1978. Columbia, SC: Foundation for American Education, 1993 ed.
Julian, George Washington. *Speeches on Political Questions.* New York, NY: Hurd and Houghton, 1872.
Kane, Joseph Nathan. *Facts About the Presidents: A Compilation of Biographical and Historical Data.* 1959. New York, NY: Ace, 1976 ed.
Kennedy, Walter Donald. *Myths of American Slavery.* Gretna, LA: Pelican Publishing Co., 2003.
Lamon, Ward Hill. *The Life of Abraham Lincoln: From His Birth to His Inauguration as President.* Boston, MA: James R. Osgood and Co., 1872.
——. *Recollections of Abraham Lincoln: 1847-1865.* Chicago, IL: A. C. McClurg and Co., 1895.
Leech, Margaret. *Reveille in Washington, 1860-1865.* 1941. Alexandria, VA: Time-Life Books, 1980 ed.
Lemire, Elise. *Black Walden: Slavery and Its Aftermath in Concord, Massachusetts.* Philadelphia, PA: University of Pennsylvania Press, 2009.
Lester, Charles Edwards. *Life and Public Services of Charles Sumner.* New York, NY: U.S. Publishing Co., 1874.
Lincoln, Abraham, and Stephen A. Douglas. *Political Debates Between Abraham Lincoln and Stephen A. Douglas.* Cleveland, OH: Burrows Brothers Co., 1894.
Litwack, Leon F. *North of Slavery: The Negro in the Free States, 1790-1860.* Chicago, IL: University of Chicago Press, 1961.
Lott, Stanley K. *The Truth About American Slavery.* 2004. Clearwater, SC: Eastern Digital Resources, 2005 ed.
McElroy, Robert. *Jefferson Davis: The Unreal and the Real.* 1937. New York, NY: Smithmark, 1995 ed.
McKissack, Patricia C., and Frederick McKissack. *Sojourner Truth: Ain't I a Woman?* New York: NY: Scholastic, 1992.
McPherson, James M. *The Atlas of the Civil War.* Philadelphia, PA: Courage Books, 2005.
Meltzer, Milton. *Slavery: A World History.* 2 vols. in 1. 1971. New York, NY: Da Capo Press, 1993 ed.
Meriwether, Elizabeth Avery. *Facts and Falsehoods Concerning the War on the South, 1861-1865.* (Originally written under the pseudonym "George Edmonds.") Memphis, TN: A. R. Taylor, 1904.
Minor, Charles Landon Carter. *The Real Lincoln: From the Testimony of His Contemporaries.* Richmond, VA: Everett Waddey Co., 1904.
Mitgang, Herbert (ed.). *Lincoln As They Saw Him.* 1956. New York, NY: Collier, 1962 ed.
Moore, George Henry. *Notes on the History of Slavery in Massachusetts.* New York, NY: D. Appleton and Co., 1866.
Mullen, Robert W. *Blacks in America's Wars: The Shift in Attitudes From the Revolutionary War to Vietnam.* 1973. New York, NY: Pathfinder, 1991 ed.
Napolitano, Andrew P. *The Constitution in Exile: How the Federal Government has Seized Power by Rewriting the Supreme Law of the Land.* Nashville, TN: Nelson Current, 2006.
Neely, Mark E., Jr. *The Fate of Liberty: Abraham Lincoln and Civil Liberties.* New York, NY: Oxford University Press, 1991.
Nicolay, John G., and John Hay (eds.). *Abraham Lincoln: A History.* 10 vols. New York, NY: The Century Co., 1890.
——. *Complete Works of Abraham Lincoln.* 12 vols. 1894. New York, NY: Francis D. Tandy Co., 1905 ed.
——. *Abraham Lincoln: Complete Works.* 12 vols. 1894. New York, NY: The Century Co., 1907 ed.
Norwood, Thomas Manson. *A True Vindication of the South.* Savannah, GA: Citizens and Southern Bank, 1917.
Nye, Russel B. *William Lloyd Garrison and the Humanitarian Reformers.* Boston, MA: Little, Brown and Co., 1955.

Oates, Stephen B. *Abraham Lincoln: The Man Behind the Myths.* New York, NY: Meridian, 1984.
ORA (full title: *The War of the Rebellion: A Compilation of the Official Records of the Union and Confederate Armies.* (Multiple volumes.) Washington, D.C.: Government Printing Office, 1880.
ORN (full title: *Official Records of the Union and Confederate Navies in the War of the Rebellion).* (Multiple volumes.) Washington, D.C.: Government Printing Office, 1894.
Owsley, Frank Lawrence. *King Cotton Diplomacy: Foreign Relations of the Confederate States of America.* 1931. Chicago, IL: University of Chicago Press, 1959 ed.
Perry, John C. *Myths and Realities of American Slavery: The True History of Slavery in America.* Shippenburg, PA: Burd Street Press, 2002.
Phillips, Wendell. *Speeches, Letters, and Lectures.* Boston, MA: Lee and Shepard, 1894.
Pickett, William Passmore. *The Negro Problem: Abraham Lincoln's Solution.* New York, NY: G. P. Putnam's Sons, 1909.
Pollard, Edward A. *Southern History of the War.* 2 vols. in 1. New York, NY: Charles B. Richardson, 1866.
———. *The Lost Cause.* 1867. Chicago, IL: E. B. Treat, 1890 ed.
———. *The Lost Cause Regained.* New York, NY: G. W. Carlton and Co., 1868.
Powell, William S. *North Carolina: A History.* 1977. Chapel Hill, NC: University of North Carolina Press, 1988 ed.
Quarles, Benjamin. *The Negro in the Civil War.* 1953. Cambridge, MA: Da Capo Press, 1988 ed.
———. *Lincoln and the Negro.* 1962. Cambridge, MA: Da Capo Press, 1990 ed.
Remsburg, John B. *Abraham Lincoln: Was He a Christian?* New York, NY: The Truth Seeker Co., 1893.
Rice, Allen Thorndike (ed.). *Reminiscences of Abraham Lincoln, by Distinguished Men of His Time.* New York, NY: North American Review, 1888.
Riley, Russell Lowell. *The Presidency and the Politics of Racial Inequality.* New York, NY: Columbia University Press, 1999.
Rosenbaum, Robert A. (ed). *The New American Desk Encyclopedia.* 1977. New York, NY: Signet, 1989 ed.
Rosenbaum, Robert A., and Douglas Brinkley (eds.). *The Penguin Encyclopedia of American History.* New York, NY: Viking, 2003.
Rutherford, Mildred Lewis. *Four Addresses.* Birmingham, AL: The Mildred Rutherford Historical Circle, 1916.
———. *A True Estimate of Abraham Lincoln and Vindication of the South.* N.p., n.d.
———. *Truths of History: A Historical Perspective of the Civil War From the Southern Viewpoint.* Confederate Reprint Co., 1920.
———. *The South Must Have Her Rightful Place In History.* Athens, GA, 1923.
Rutland, Robert Allen. *The Birth of the Bill of Rights, 1776-1791.* 1955. Boston, MA: Northeastern University Press, 1991 ed.
Seabrook, Lochlainn. *Carnton Plantation Ghost Stories: True Tales of the Unexplained from Tennessee's Most Haunted Civil War House!* 2005. Franklin, TN, 2016 ed.
———. *Nathan Bedford Forrest: Southern Hero, American Patriot.* 2007. Franklin, TN, 2010 ed.
———. *Abraham Lincoln: The Southern View.* 2007. Franklin, TN: Sea Raven Press, 2013 ed.
———. *The McGavocks of Carnton Plantation: A Southern History - Celebrating One of Dixie's Most Noble Confederate Families and Their Tennessee Home.* 2008. Franklin, TN, 2011ed.
———. *A Rebel Born: A Defense of Nathan Bedford Forrest.* 2010. Franklin, TN: Sea Raven Press, 2011 ed.
———. *A Rebel Born: The Screenplay* (for the film). 2011. Franklin, TN: Sea Raven Press.
———. *Everything You Were Taught About the Civil War is Wrong, Ask a Southerner!* 2010. Franklin, TN: Sea Raven Press, revised 2014 ed.
———. *The Quotable Jefferson Davis: Selections From the Writings and Speeches of the Confederacy's First President.* Franklin, TN: Sea Raven Press, 2011.
———. *The Quotable Robert E. Lee: Selections From the Writings and Speeches of the South's Most Beloved Civil War General.* Franklin, TN: Sea Raven Press, 2011 Sesquicentennial Civil War Edition.
———. *Lincolnology: The Real Abraham Lincoln Revealed In His Own Words.* Franklin, TN: Sea Raven Press, 2011.
———. *Honest Jeff and Dishonest Abe: A Southern Children's Guide to the Civil War.* Franklin, TN: Sea Raven Press, 2012.
———. *Encyclopedia of the Battle of Franklin - A Comprehensive Guide to the Conflict that Changed the Civil War.* Franklin, TN: Sea Raven Press, 2012.
———. *The Quotable Nathan Bedford Forrest: Selections From the Writings and Speeches of the Confederacy's Most Brilliant Cavalryman.* Spring Hill, TN: Sea Raven Press, 2012.
———. *Forrest! 99 Reasons to Love Nathan Bedford Forrest.* Spring Hill, TN: Sea Raven Press, 2012.
———. *Give 'Em Hell Boys! The Complete Military Correspondence of Nathan Bedford Forrest.* Spring Hill, TN: Sea Raven Press, 2012.
———. *The Constitution of the Confederate States of America Explained: A Clause-by-Clause Study of the South's Magna Carta.* Spring Hill, TN: Sea Raven Press, 2012 Sesquicentennial Civil War Edition.
———. *The Great Impersonator: 99 Reasons to Dislike Abraham Lincoln.* Spring Hill, TN: Sea Raven Press, 2012.
———. *The Old Rebel: Robert E. Lee As He Was Seen By His Contemporaries.* Spring Hill, TN: Sea Raven Press, 2012 Sesquicentennial Civil War Edition.
———. *The Quotable Stonewall Jackson: Selections From the Writings and Speeches of the South's Most Famous General.* Spring Hill, TN: Sea Raven Press, 2012 Sesquicentennial Civil War Edition.
———. *Saddle, Sword, and Gun: A Biography of Nathan Bedford Forrest for Teens.* Spring Hill, TN: Sea Raven Press, 2013.
———. *The Alexander H. Stephens Reader: Excerpts From the Works of a Confederate Founding Father.* Spring Hill, TN: Sea Raven Press, 2013.
———. *The Quotable Alexander H. Stephens: Selections From the Writings and Speeches of the Confederacy's First Vice President.* Spring Hill, TN: Sea Raven Press, 2013 Sesquicentennial Civil War Edition.
———. *Give This Book to a Yankee! A Southern Guide to the Civil War for Northerners.* Spring Hill, TN: Sea Raven Press, 2014.

——. *The Articles of Confederation Explained: A Clause-by-Clause Study of America's First Constitution*. Spring Hill, TN: Sea Raven Press, 2014.
——. *Confederate Blood and Treasure: An Interview With Lochlainn Seabrook*. Spring Hill, TN: Sea Raven Press, 2015.
——. *Nathan Bedford Forrest and the Battle of Fort Pillow: Yankee Myth, Confederate Fact*. Spring Hill, TN: Sea Raven Press, 2015.
——. *Everything You Were Taught About American Slavery War is Wrong, Ask a Southerner!* Spring Hill, TN: Sea Raven Press, 2015.
——. *Confederacy 101: Amazing Facts You Never Knew About America's Oldest Political Tradition*. Spring Hill, TN: Sea Raven Press, 2015.
——. *The Great Yankee Coverup: What the North Doesn't Want You to Know About Lincoln's War!* Spring Hill, TN: Sea Raven Press, 2015.
——. *Slavery 101: Amazing Facts You Never Knew About America's "Peculiar Institution."* Spring Hill, TN: Sea Raven Press, 2015.
——. *Confederate Flag Facts: What Every American Should Know About Dixie's Southern Cross*. Spring Hill, TN: Sea Raven Press, 2016.
——. *Nathan Bedford Forrest and the Ku Klux Klan: Yankee Myth, Confederate Fact*. Spring Hill, TN: Sea Raven Press, 2016.
——. *Seabrook's Bible Dictionary of Traditional and Mystical Christian Doctrines*. Spring Hill, TN: Sea Raven Press, 2016.
——. *Everything You Were Taught About African-Americans and the Civil War is Wrong, Ask a Southerner!* Spring Hill, TN: Sea Raven Press, 2016.
——. *Nathan Bedford Forrest and African-Americans: Yankee Myth, Confederate Fact*. Spring Hill, TN: Sea Raven Press, 2016.
——. *Women in Gray: A Tribute to the Ladies Who Supported the Southern Confederacy*. Spring Hill, TN: Sea Raven Press, 2016.
——. *Lincoln's War: The Real Cause, the Real Winner, the Real Loser*. Spring Hill, TN: Sea Raven Press, 2016.
——. *The Unholy Crusade: Lincoln's Legacy of Destruction in the American South*. Spring Hill, TN: Sea Raven Press, 2017.
——. *Abraham Lincoln Was a Liberal, Jefferson Davis Was a Conservative: The Missing Key to Understanding the American Civil War*. Spring Hill, TN: Sea Raven Press, 2017.
——. *All We Ask is to be Let Alone: The Southern Secession Fact Book*. Spring Hill, TN: Sea Raven Press, 2017.
——. *The Ultimate Civil War Quiz Book: How Much Do You Really Know About America's Most Misunderstood Conflict?* Spring Hill, TN: Sea Raven Press, 2017.
——. *Rise Up and Call Them Blessed: Victorian Tributes to the Confederate Soldier, 1861-1901*. Spring Hill, TN: Sea Raven Press, 2017.
——. *Victorian Confederate Poetry: The Southern Cause in Verse, 1861-1901*. Spring Hill, TN: Sea Raven Press, 2018.
Shotwell, Walter G. *Life of Charles Sumner*. New York, NY: Thomas Y. Crowell and Co., 1910.
Simpson, Lewis P. (ed.). *I'll Take My Stand: The South and the Agrarian Tradition*. 1930. Baton Rouge, LA: University of Louisiana Press, 1977 ed.
Smith, Mark M. (ed.). *The Old South*. Oxford, UK: Blackwell Publishers, 2001.
Stephens, Alexander Hamilton. *Speech of Mr. Stephens, of Georgia, on the War and Taxation*. Washington, D.C.: J & G. Gideon, 1848.
——. *A Constitutional View of the Late War Between the States; Its Causes, Character, Conduct and Results*. 2 vols. Philadelphia, PA: National Publishing, Co., 1870.
——. *Recollections of Alexander H. Stephens: His Diary Kept When a Prisoner at Fort Warren, Boston Harbour, 1865*. New York, NY: Doubleday, Page, and Co., 1910.
Tagg, Larry. *The Unpopular Mr. Lincoln: The Story of America's Most Reviled President*. New York, NY: Savas Beatie, 2009.
Tatalovich, Raymond, and Byron W. Daynes. *Presidential Power in the United States*. Monterey, CA: Brooks/Cole, 1984.
The Congressional Globe, Containing Sketches of the Debates and Proceedings of the First Session of the Twenty-Eighth Congress (Vol. 13). Washington, D.C.: The Globe, 1844.
The National Almanac and Annual Record for the Year 1863. Philadelphia, PA: George W. Childs, 1863.
Thornton, Mark, and Robert B. Ekelund, Jr. *Tariffs, Blockades, and Inflation: The Economics of the Civil War*. Wilmington, DE: Scholarly Resources, 2004.
Tracy, Gilbert A. (ed.). *Uncollected Letters of Abraham Lincoln*. Boston, MA: Houghton Mifflin Co., 1917.
Villard, Henry. *Memoirs of Henry Villard, Journalist and Financier, 1835-1900*. 2 vols. Boston, MA: Houghton, Mifflin and Co., 1904.
Wallechinsky, David, Irving Wallace, and Amy Wallace. *The People's Almanac Presents The Book of Lists*. New York, NY: Morrow, 1977.
Weintraub, Max. *The Blue Book of American History*. New York, NY: Regents Publishing Co., 1960.
Wiley, Bell Irvin. *Southern Negroes: 1861-1865*. 1938. New Haven, CT: Yale University Press, 1969 ed.
Wilson, Woodrow. *Division and Reunion: 1829-1889*. 1893. New York, NY: Longmans, Green, and Co., 1908 ed.
Woods, Thomas E., Jr. *The Politically Incorrect Guide to American History*. Washington, D.C.: Regnery, 2004.

∽ MEET THE AUTHOR ∽

"DEMANDING THE PATRIOTIC SOUTH TO STOP HONORING HER CONFEDERATE ANCESTORS IS LIKE DEMANDING THE SUN NOT TO SHINE." — COLONEL LOCHLAINN SEABROOK

LOCHLAINN SEABROOK, a neo-Victorian and world acclaimed man of letters, is a Kentucky Colonel and the winner of the prestigious Jefferson Davis Historical Gold Medal for his "masterpiece," *A Rebel Born: A Defense of Nathan Bedford Forrest*. A classic littérateur and an unreconstructed Southern historian, he is an award-winning author, Civil War scholar, Confederate culture expert, Bible authority, the leading popularizer of American Civil War history, and a traditional Southern Agrarian of Scottish, English, Irish, Dutch, Welsh, German, and Italian extraction.

A child prodigy, Seabrook is today a true Renaissance Man whose occupational titles also include encyclopedist, lexicographer, musician, artist, graphic designer, genealogist, photographer, and award-winning poet. Also a songwriter and a screenwriter, he has a 40 year background in historical nonfiction writing and is a member of the Sons of Confederate Veterans, the Civil War Trust, and the National Grange.

Known to his many fans as the "voice of the traditional South," due to similarities in their writing styles, ideas, and literary works, Seabrook is also often referred to as the "new Shelby Foote," the "Southern Joseph Campbell," and the "American Robert Graves" (his English cousin). Seabrook coined the terms "South-shaming" and "Lincolnian liberalism," and holds the world's record for writing the most books on Nathan Bedford Forrest: nine. In addition, Seabrook is the first Civil War scholar to connect the early American nickname for the U.S., "The Confederate States of America," with the Southern Confederacy that arose eight decades later, and the first to note that in 1860 the party platforms of the two major political parties were the opposite of what they are today (Victorian Democrats were conservatives, Victorian Republicans were liberals).

The grandson of an Appalachian coal-mining family, Seabrook is a seventh-generation Kentuckian whose European ancestors came from Virginia, North Carolina, and Tennessee, settling in the Bluegrass State in the early 1700s, thereafter spreading into West Virginia and the Midwest.

Above, Colonel Lochlainn Seabrook, "the voice of the traditional South," award-winning Civil War scholar and unreconstructed Southern historian. America's most popular and prolific pro-South author, his many books have introduced hundreds of thousands to the truth about the War for Southern Independence. He coined the phrase "South-shaming" and holds the world record for writing the most books on Nathan Bedford Forrest: nine.

Seabrook is co-chair of the Jent/Gent Family Committee (Kentucky), founder and director of the Blakeney Family Tree Project, and a board member of the Friends of Colonel Benjamin E. Caudill. His literary works have been endorsed by leading authorities, museum curators, award-winning historians, bestselling authors, celebrities, noted scientists, well regarded educators, TV show hosts and producers, renowned military artists, esteemed Southern organizations, and distinguished academicians from around the world.

Seabrook has authored over 50 popular adult books on the American Civil War, American and international slavery, the U.S. Confederacy (1781), the Southern Confederacy (1861), religion, theology, thealogy, Jesus, the Bible, the Apocrypha, the Law of Attraction, alternative health, spirituality, ghost stories, the paranormal, ufology, social issues, and cross-cultural studies of the family and marriage. His Confederate biographies, pro-South studies, genealogical monographs, family histories, military encyclopedias, self-help guides, and etymological dictionaries have received wide acclaim.

Seabrook's eight children's books include a Southern guide to the Civil War, a biography of Nathan Bedford Forrest, a dictionary of religion and myth, a rewriting of the King Arthur legend (which reinstates the original pre-Christian motifs), two bedtime stories for preschoolers, a naturalist's guidebook to owls, a worldwide look at the family, and an examination of the Near-Death Experience.

Of blue-blooded Southern stock through his Kentucky, Tennessee, Virginia, North Carolina and West Virginia ancestors, he is a direct descendant of European royalty via his 6th great-grandfather, the Earl of Oxford, after which London's famous Harley Street is named. Among his celebrated male Celtic ancestors is Robert the Bruce, King of Scotland, Seabrook's 22nd great-grandfather. The 21st great-grandson of Edward I "Longshanks" Plantagenet), King of England, Seabrook is a thirteenth-generation Southerner through his descent from the colonists of Jamestown, Virginia (1607).

The 2nd, 3rd, and 4th great-grandson of dozens of Confederate soldiers, one of his closest connections to Lincoln's War is through his 3rd great-grandfather, Elias Jent, Sr., who fought for the Confederacy in the Thirteenth Cavalry Kentucky under Seabrook's 2nd cousin, Colonel Benjamin E. Caudill. The Thirteenth, also known as "Caudill's Army," fought in numerous conflicts, including the Battles of Saltville, Gladsville, Mill Cliff, Poor Fork, Whitesburg, and Leatherwood.

Seabrook is a direct descendant of the families of Alexander H. Stephens, John Singleton Mosby, William Giles Harding, and Edmund Winchester Rucker, and is related to the following Confederates and other 18th- and 19th-Century luminaries: Robert E. Lee, Stephen Dill Lee, Stonewall Jackson, Nathan Bedford Forrest, James Longstreet, John Hunt Morgan, Jeb Stuart, Pierre G. T. Beauregard (approved the Confederate Battle Flag design), George W. Gordon, John Bell Hood, Alexander Peter Stewart, Arthur M. Manigault, Joseph Manigault, Charles Scott Venable, Thornton A. Washington, John A. Washington, Abraham Buford, Edmund W. Pettus, Theodrick "Tod" Carter, John B. Womack, John H. Winder, Gideon J. Pillow, States Rights Gist, Henry R. Jackson, John Lawton Seabrook, John C. Breckinridge, Leonidas Polk, Zachary Taylor, Sarah Knox Taylor (first wife of Jefferson Davis), Richard Taylor, Davy Crockett, Daniel Boone, Meriwether Lewis (of the Lewis and Clark Expedition) Andrew Jackson, James K. Polk, Abram Poindexter Maury (founder of Franklin, TN), Zebulon Vance, Thomas Jefferson, Edmund Jennings Randolph, George Wythe Randolph (grandson of Jefferson), Felix K. Zollicoffer, Fitzhugh Lee, Nathaniel F. Cheairs, Jesse James, Frank James, Robert Brank Vance, Charles Sidney Winder, John W. McGavock, Caroline E. (Winder) McGavock, David Harding McGavock, Lysander McGavock, James Randal McGavock, Randall William McGavock, Francis McGavock, Emily McGavock, William Henry F. Lee, Lucius E. Polk, Minor Meriwether (husband of noted pro-South author Elizabeth Avery Meriwether), Ellen Bourne Tynes (wife of Forrest's chief of artillery, Captain John W. Morton), South Carolina Senators Preston Smith Brooks and Andrew Pickens Butler, and famed South Carolina diarist Mary Chesnut.

Seabrook's modern day cousins include: Patrick J. Buchanan (conservative author), Cindy Crawford (model), Shelby Lee Adams (Letcher Co., Kentucky, photographer), Bertram Thomas Combs (Kentucky's 50th governor), Edith Bolling (wife of President Woodrow Wilson), and actors Andy Griffith, Riley Keough, George C. Scott, Robert Duvall, Reese Witherspoon, Lee Marvin, Rebecca Gayheart, and Tom Cruise.

Seabrook's screenplay, *A Rebel Born*, based on his book of the same name, has been signed with acclaimed filmmaker Christopher Forbes (of Forbes Film). It is now in pre-production, and is set for release in 2018 as a full-length feature film. This will be the first movie ever made of Nathan Bedford Forrest's life story, and as a historically accurate project written from the Southern perspective, is destined to be one of the most talked about Civil War films of all time.

Born with music in his blood, Seabrook is an award-winning, multi-genre, BMI-Nashville songwriter and lyricist who has composed some 3,000 songs (250 albums), and whose original music has been heard in film (*A Rebel Born, Cowgirls 'n Angels, Confederate Cavalry, Billy the Kid: Showdown in Lincoln County, Vengeance Without Mercy, Last Step, County Line, The Mark*) and on TV and radio worldwide. A musician, producer, multi-instrumentalist, and renown performer—whose keyboard work has been variously compared to pianists from Hargus Robbins and Vince Guaraldi to Elton John and Leonard Bernstein—Seabrook has opened for groups such as the Earl Scruggs Review, Ted Nugent, and Bob Seger, and has performed privately for such public figures as President Ronald Reagan, Burt Reynolds, Loni Anderson, and Senator Edward W. Brooke. Seabrook's cousins in the music business include: Johnny Cash, Elvis Presley, Lisa Marie Presley, Billy Ray and Miley Cyrus, Patty Loveless, Tim McGraw, Lee Ann Womack, Dolly Parton, Pat Boone, Naomi, Wynonna, and Ashley Judd, Ricky Skaggs, the Sunshine Sisters, Martha Carson, and Chet Atkins.

Seabrook lives with his wife and family in historic Middle Tennessee, the heart of Forrest country and the Confederacy, where his conservative Southern ancestors fought valiantly against Liberal Lincoln and the progressive North in defense of Jeffersonianism, constitutional government, and personal liberty.

LochlainnSeabrook.com

Meet the Cover Artist

CHRISTOPHER ROMMEL is an award-winning Master Caricaturist and freelance illustrator who has been drawing ever since he was old enough to hold a pencil. He is the founder and owner of Exaggerated Entertainment, through which he serves as a party caricaturist for all types of events, including holiday parties, company picnics, birthdays, anniversaries, bar/bat mitzvahs, confirmations, wedding receptions, reunions, banquets, proms, student lock-ins, graduations, open houses, grand openings, trade shows, conventions, conferences, concerts, fund raisers, and boat cruises.

A member of the International Society of Caricature Artists, Rommel won the organization's prestigious "Golden Nosey" award (the Oscar of the caricature industry) for Caricaturist of the Year in 2006. The recipient of numerous other awards for such likenesses as Donald Trump and Christopher Reeve, he is also a nationally published illustrator whose work has appeared in a variety of periodicals and publications, such as *Playboy*, *FHM*, *Flex*, *Exaggerated Features*, and Sea Raven Press.

(Illustration © Chris Rommel)

Rommel launched his career as a professional caricature artist in 1998 when he applied for a summer job at Valleyfair Amusement Park in Shakopee, Minnesota. While employed there he came under the tutelage of renowned *MAD Magazine* artist Tom Richmond. His enrollment at the Academy of Art University in San Francisco, California, as well as two Wisconsin state universities, educated him in a variety of art concentrations. He earned a Bachelor of Fine Arts degree from the University of Wisconsin-Eau Claire in 1999.

Since then, Rommel has drawn some 50,000 live caricatures of people at amusement parks, state fairs, shopping malls, corporate events and private parties. Among his better known clients are Harley-Davidson, Applebee's, Bank of America, Pillsbury, Mars Chocolate, Wells Fargo, First Bank and Trust, Hormel Foods, Petco, Absolut Vodka, Boston Scientific, Walmart and The Home Depot.

Rommel currently resides in Eau Claire, Wisconsin, where he continues to develop both his craft and his well deserved reputation as one of America's premier artists.

ChrisRommel.com

The Unquotable Abraham Lincoln

"What I would most desire would be the separation of the white and black races." July 17, 1858, Springfield, Illinois

150 ∽ THE UNQUOTABLE ABRAHAM LINCOLN

If you enjoyed this book you will be interested in Colonel Seabrook's other popular related titles:

- EVERYTHING YOU WERE TAUGHT ABOUT THE CIVIL WAR IS WRONG, ASK A SOUTHERNER!
- ABRAHAM LINCOLN WAS A LIBERAL, JEFFERSON DAVIS WAS A CONSERVATIVE
- ALL WE ASK IS TO BE LET ALONE: THE SOUTHERN SECESSION FACT BOOK
- EVERYTHING YOU WERE TAUGHT ABOUT AMERICAN SLAVERY IS WRONG, ASK A SOUTHERNER!
- CONFEDERATE FLAG FACTS: WHAT EVERY AMERICAN SHOULD KNOW ABOUT DIXIE'S SOUTHERN CROSS
- LINCOLN'S WAR: THE REAL CAUSE, THE REAL WINNER, THE REAL LOSER

Available from Sea Raven Press and wherever fine books are sold

  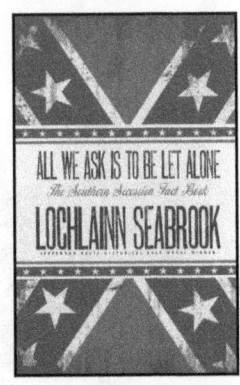

ALL OF OUR BOOK COVERS ARE AVAILABLE AS 11" X 17" POSTERS, SUITABLE FOR FRAMING

SeaRavenPress.com • NathanBedfordForrestBooks.com

www.ingramcontent.com/pod-product-compliance
Lightning Source LLC
LaVergne TN
LVHW090116080426
835507LV00040B/919